Depression and Bipolar Disorder

Psychological Disorders

Psychological
Disorders

Depression and Bipolar Disorder

Vatsal G. Thakkar, M.D.

Series Editor
Christine Collins, Ph.D.

Foreword by
Pat Levitt, Ph.D.
Vanderbilt Kennedy
Center for Research
on Human Development

CHELSEA HOUSE
PUBLISHERS
An imprint of Infobase Publishing

Depression and Bipolar Disorder

Chelsea House
An imprint of Infobase Publishing
132 West 31st Street
New York NY 10001

ISBN-10: 0-7910-8542-2
ISBN-13: 978-0-7910-8542-4

Library of Congress Cataloging-in-Publication Data
Thakkar, Vatsal, 1972-
  Depression and bipolar disorder / Vatsal Thakkar.
     p. cm. — (Psychological disorders)
  Includes bibliographical references and index.
  ISBN 0-7910-8542-2
  1. Affective disorders—Juvenile literature. 2. Depression, Mental—Juvenile
literature. 3. Manic depressive illness—Juvenile literature.
  I. Title. II. Psychological disorders (Chelsea House Publishers)
  RC537.T475 2006
  616.85'27—dc22   2005026486

Chelsea House books are available at special discounts when purchased in bulk quantities for businesses, associations, institutions, or sales promotions. Please call our Special Sales Department in New York at (212) 967-8800 or (800) 322-8755.

You can find Chelsea House on the World Wide Web at http://www.chelseahouse.com

Text and cover design by Keith Trego

Printed in the United States of America

Bang EJB 10 9 8 7 6 5 4 3 2

This book is printed on acid-free paper.

All links and web addresses were checked and verified to be correct at the time of publication. Because of the dynamic nature of the web, some addresses and links may have changed since publication and may no longer be valid.

Table of
Contents

Foreword

Pat Levitt, Ph.D.
Kennedy Center for Research
on Human Development
Vanderbilt University

Think of the most complicated aspect of our universe, and then multiply that by infinity! Even the most enthusiastic of mathematicians and physicists acknowledge that the brain is by far the most challenging entity to understand. By design, the human brain is made up of billions of cells called neurons, which use chemical neurotransmitters to communicate with each other through connections called synapses. Each brain cell has about 2,000 synapses. Connections between neurons are not formed in a random fashion, but rather, are organized into a type of architecture that is far more complex than any of today's supercomputers. And, not only is the brain's connective architecture more complex than any computer, its connections are capable of *changing* to improve the way a circuit functions. For example, the way we learn new information involves changes in circuits that actually improve performance. Yet some change can also result in a disruption of connections, like changes that occur in disorders such as drug addiction, depression, schizophrenia, and epilepsy, or even changes that can increase a person's risk of suicide.

Genes and the environment are powerful forces in building the brain during development and ensuring normal brain functioning, but they can also be the root causes of psychological and neurological disorders when things go awry. The way in which brain architecture is built before birth and in childhood will determine how well the brain functions when we are adults, and even how susceptible we are to such diseases as depression, anxiety, or attention disorders, which can severely disturb brain function. In a sense, then, understanding how the brain is built can lead us to a clearer picture of the ways in which our brain works, how we can improve its functioning, and what we can do to repair it when diseases strike.

Brain architecture reflects the highly specialized jobs that are performed by human beings, such as seeing, hearing, feeling, smelling, and moving. Different brain areas are specialized to control specific functions. Each specialized area must communicate well with other areas for the brain to accomplish even more complex tasks, like controlling body physiology—our patterns of sleep, for example, or even our eating habits, both of which can become disrupted if brain development or function is disturbed in some way. The brain controls our feelings, fears, and emotions; our ability to learn and store new information; and how well we recall old information. The brain does all this, and more, by building, during development, the circuits that control these functions, much like a hard-wired computer. Even small abnormalities that occur during early brain development through gene mutations, viral infection, or fetal exposure to alcohol can increase the risk of developing a wide range of psychological disorders later in life.

Those who study the relationship between brain architecture and function, and the diseases that affect this bond, are neuroscientists. Those who study and treat the disorders that are caused by changes in brain architecture and chemistry are psychiatrists and psychologists. Over the last 50 years, we have learned quite a lot about how brain architecture and chemistry work and how genetics contribute to brain structure and function. Genes are very important in controlling the initial phases of building the brain. In fact, almost every gene in the human genome is needed to build the brain. This process of brain development actually starts prior to birth, with almost all the neurons we will ever have in our brain produced by mid-gestation. The assembly of the architecture, in the form of intricate circuits, begins by this time, and by birth, we have the basic organization laid out. But the work is not yet complete, because billions of connections form over a remarkably long period of time, extending through puberty. The brain of a child is being built and modified on a daily basis, even during sleep.

While there are thousands of chemical building blocks, such as proteins, lipids, and carbohydrates, that are used, much like bricks and mortar, to put the architecture together, the highly detailed connectivity that emerges during childhood depends greatly upon experiences and our environment. In building a house, we use specific blueprints to assemble the basic structures, like a foundation, walls, floors, and ceilings. The brain is assembled similarly. Plumbing and electricity, like the basic circuitry of the brain, are put in place early in the building process. But for all of this early work, there is another very important phase of development, which is termed experience-dependent development. During the first three years of life, our brains actually form far more connections than we will ever need, almost 40% more! Why would this occur? Well, in fact, the early circuits form in this way so that we can use experience to mold our brain architecture to best suit the functions that we are likely to need for the rest of our lives.

Experience is not just important for the circuits that control our senses. A young child who experiences toxic stress, like physical abuse, will have his or her brain architecture changed in regions that will result in poorer control of emotions and feelings as an adult. Experience is powerful. When we repeatedly practice on the piano or shoot a basketball hundreds of times daily, we are using experience to model our brain connections to function at their finest. Some will achieve better results than others, perhaps because the initial phases of circuit-building provided a better base, just like the architecture of houses may differ in terms of their functionality. We are working to understand the brain structure and function that result from the powerful combination of genes building the initial architecture and a child's experience adding the all-important detailed touches. We also know that, like an old home, the architecture can break down. The aging process can be particularly hard on the ability of brain circuits to function at their best because positive change comes less readily as we get older. Synapses may be lost and brain chemistry can change over time. The difficulties in understanding how architecture gets built are paralleled by the complexities of what happens to that architecture as we grow older. Dementia associated with brain deterioration as a complication of Alzheimer's disease, or memory loss associated with aging or alcoholism are active avenues of research in the neuroscience community.

There is truth, both for development and in aging, in the old adage "use it or lose it." Neuroscientists are pursuing the idea that brain architecture and chemistry can be modified well beyond childhood. If we understand the mechanisms that make it easy for a young, healthy brain to learn or repair itself following an accident, perhaps we can use those same tools to optimize the functioning of aging brains. We already know many ways in which we can improve the functioning of the aging or injured brain. For example, for an individual who has suffered a stroke that has caused structural damage to brain architecture, physical exercise can be quite powerful in helping to reorganize circuits so that they function better, even in an elderly individual. And you know that when you exercise and sleep regularly, you just feel better. Your brain chemistry and architecture are functioning at their best. Another example of ways we can improve nervous system function are the drugs that are used to treat mental illnesses. These drugs are designed to change brain chemistry so that the neurotransmitters used for communication between brain cells can function more normally. These same types of drugs, however, when taken in excess or abused, can actually damage brain chemistry and change brain architecture so that it functions more poorly.

As you read the series Psychological Disorders, the images of altered brain organization and chemistry will come to mind in thinking about complex diseases such as schizophrenia or drug addiction. There is nothing more fascinating and important to understand for the well-being of humans. But also keep in mind that as neuroscientists, we are on a mission to comprehend human nature, the way we perceive the world, how we recognize color, why we smile when thinking about the Thanksgiving turkey, the emotion of experiencing our first kiss, or how we can remember the winner of the 1953 World Series. If you are interested in people, and the world in which we live, you are a neuroscientist, too.

Pat Levitt, Ph.D.
Director, Vanderbilt Kennedy Center
for Research on Human Development
Vanderbilt University
Nashville, Tennessee

Introduction

Changing moods are nothing unusual. Everyone experiences them. Everyday life creates moods that can be happy, sad, angry, irritable, and indifferent; the list goes on and on. Moods are something that everyone has. Most of us react normally to our moods—that is, different events bring about changes of mood that, over time, go back to our normal baseline, or usual, mood. Most people, most of the time, feel that they are in control of their moods. Even when their moods wander away from their baseline, they are confident that they will eventually return to normal (Figure 1.1).

When we discuss mood disorders, we are referring to conditions in which a person's mood may either start from a place that is very different from the usual concept of what a "normal mood" is, or a condition where someone's mood, after reacting to a stressor, may not return to baseline for weeks, months, or even years. We are talking about inappropriately and excessively low moods (as seen with **major depressive episode** and **major depressive disorder**), or inappropriately and excessively elevated moods (as in the manic phase of bipolar disorder, which is sometimes called manic-depressive illness or manic depression).

MOOD DISORDERS THROUGHOUT HISTORY
Evidence of severe mood disturbances has existed throughout history. What has changed through the years, however, is how

Normal Fluctuations of Mood

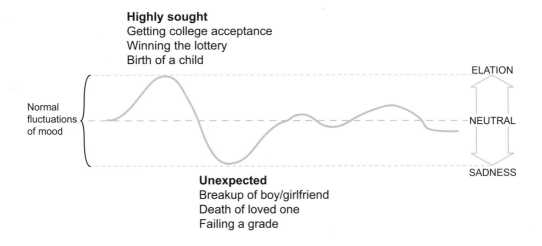

Figure 1.1 Mood fluctuations are normal. Accomplishing highly sought goals or wishes causes elation. Unexpected obstacles such as the breakup of a relationship lower can cause deep sadness.

these disturbances are viewed and what they are called. Hippocrates, an ancient Greek physician now known as the Father of Medicine, lived from about 460 to 377 B.C. He used the terms *mania* and **melancholia** to describe different types of mental illness. He was also one of the first people to believe that things like thought, ideas, and feelings came from the brain and not the heart. The terms and ideas he introduced are still used today. There are references to mood disorders as far back as the Old Testament story of King Saul and Homer's *Iliad*. In fact, the term *melancholy*, meaning "sadness" or "gloom," comes from the term *melancholia*, an ancient description of depressive illness by Roman physician Aulus

What Is Normal?

Throughout history, society has struggled to define what *normal* means. What is "normal?" How do we define *normality*? The medical model of normalcy subdivides different biological characteristics and examines them within a large population. This is how we find out how certain characteristics are distributed among a population. Let's use height as an example, looking at men. We can calculate the average height, which would be around 5 feet, 10 inches. Furthermore, we can determine that those under 5 feet, 3 inches and those over 6 feet, 3 inches are in the minority. The vast majority of men fall somewhere between these two heights. This concept is called a Gaussian distribution (Figure 1.2). Medicine uses these sorts of statistics, in part, to define what is normal.

Just as many biological characteristics can be plotted according to the Gaussian distribution, so can certain elements of psychological functioning. Most people use the term *mood* as a description of their emotional state at a given moment or on a given day. In psychiatric terms, however, when we discuss mood disorders, we look not only at mood but also at mood-related functions such as energy level, appetite, sleep, and concentration. We refer to a normal mood state as euthymic. Mood disorders are conditions that cause more than one of these biological and psychological functions to be disrupted for a prolonged period of time, resulting in dysfunction at work, school, or in social situations.[1]

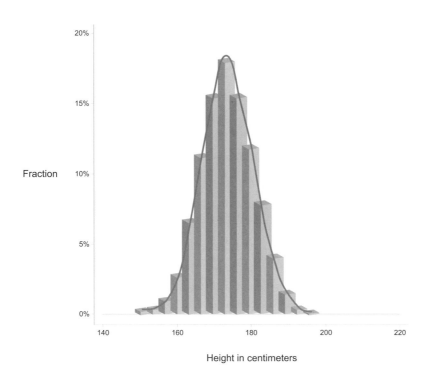

Figure 1.2 Gaussian distribution curve is shown above.

Cornelius Celsus (*melan* = "black" and *cholé* = "bile"). Ancient medical theory was based on the principle that there were four humors, or bodily fluids: blood, phlegm, yellow bile, and black bile. The thinking at the time was that depression was caused by an excess of black bile. It wasn't until the nineteenth century that physicians discovered that periods of mania and depression can occur as part of the same disorder. Building on the work of psychiatrists before him, German psychiatrist Emil Kraepelin

(1856–1926) was one of the first physicians to distinguish manic psychosis, one of the most severe and debilitating forms of mania, from severe psychiatric condition, dementia precox (now known as **schizophrenia**). His description of mania continues to form the basis for our diagnostic criteria today.

THE CHANGING FACE OF MOOD DISORDERS

The National Institutes of Mental Health (NIMH) reports that in any given year, 18 million people will suffer from **clinical depression**. Of these, 3 million are children and adolescents under the age of 18. As the science of **psychiatry** has progressed, so has society's acceptance of mood disorders. **Antidepressant** medications to combat depression are now advertised on television, and seeking treatment for a mood disorder from a mental health professional is no longer stigmatized. In recent years, a number of public figures have disclosed their own struggles with mood disorders. A few famous entertainers who have admitted to battling clinical depression include Drew Carey (actor and comedian), Sheryl Crow (singer/songwriter, Figure 1.3), and George Stephanopoulis (former advisor to President Bill Clinton and now an ABC television news host). Some well-known people who have publicly disclosed their struggle with bipolar disorder include Jane Pauley (former NBC *Dateline* host), Buzz Aldrin (astronaut), and one of the most successful entrepreneurs of all time, Ted Turner (founder of CNN and the Turner cable networks). As you can see, suffering from a mood disorder did not hold these people back, although it may have made their road to success somewhat more challenging. Mood disorders such as major depressive disorder and bipolar disorder can affect anyone from any walk of life, but with appropriate treatment, people can manage these disorders.

Figure 1.3 Many famous celebrities, such as singer/songwriter Sheryl Crow, have battled clinical depression.

SYMPTOMS OF MOOD DISORDERS

Before we can define the different mood disorders, we must first identify the different mood states that make them up. The information used to help define and diagnose both mood episodes and mood disorders is found in the *Diagnostic and Statistical Manual of Mental Disorders,* 4th edition (DSM-IV), published by the American Psychiatric Association (APA). If we think of the mood spectrum as having two poles, the "low" pole would be sadness and the "high" pole would be **elation**. These are the two areas in which a mood disorder can manifest. Excessive or inappropriate sadness (or lack of interest), along with other associated symptoms, is characteristic of a depressive disorder. Other symptoms may include **insomnia**, loss of appetite, and **lethargy**. Excessive elation, and **euphoria**, along

What Is Psychiatry?

Psychiatry is the medical specialty that deals with psychological functioning and health. It is the invisible science of the intangible—things that cannot be measured by a ruler, a scale, a blood test, or an X-ray. Psychiatry involves the science of observing and measuring aspects of psychological functioning against a norm. We must be careful not to overlabel or overdiagnose anything that we deem to be outside the norm. After all, people may be as different from "normal" as they wish. As long as they are not endangering themselves or anyone else, they should not be viewed as having a mental health problem. Because psychiatry is so intangible, it is susceptible to differences of opinion, even among mental health professionals. Therefore, this art within a science has often been mired in controversy. Perhaps one day in the future, we will be able to perform a complex brain scan that can diagnose mental illness, but for now, we have to do it the old-fashioned way—by history, observation, and interview.

with other associated symptoms—such as hyperactivity, less need for sleep, and **flight of ideas**—are characteristic of mania. Mania is the distinguishing feature of bipolar disorder, which includes fluctuating mood symptoms from both poles: sadness and elation. This book will explore both depression and bipolar disorder, looking at the causes, symptoms, and treatments associated with these mood disorders.

The Depressive Disorders

There are three main types of depressive mood disorders. The first is major depressive disorder, which can cover a broad spectrum of symptoms. The second one is dysthymic disorder, which is considered a milder but chronic (long-lasting) disorder. Finally, there are other depressive syndromes, which will be discussed in Chapter 4, that don't fit into these two categories. It is important to remember that to be diagnosed with any of these three types of depressive disorders, a person must experience **dysfunction** in social situations, school, or work as a result of the symptoms.

MAJOR DEPRESSIVE DISORDER

Major Depressive Episode

A major depressive episode (MDE) is at the core of major depressive disorder. This is an episode in which various neurological, psychological, and physical symptoms of depression are experienced for at least most of the day, every day, for a duration of *at least two weeks*. One of these symptoms must include either a depressed mood or seriously diminished interest, although both can occur at the same time. Other symptoms include a sharp change in appetite or sleep patterns, excessive **fatigue**, significant change in weight (usually a loss of weight), feelings of worthlessness or guilt, difficulty concentrating, and recurrent thoughts of death or suicide.

It is important to keep in mind that a person doesn't have to have *all* of these symptoms to experience major depression. He or she may have just two or three severe symptoms that demand professional help. However, five or more of the symptoms must occur for major depressive episode to be diagnosed.

Major Depressive Disorder

Gina was a 17-year-old high school senior who was referred for psychiatric evaluation after she attempted suicide by taking an overdose of pills. On the night of the suicide attempt, she had a fight with her mother. Gina remembered her mother saying that she was a "spoiled brat" and asking whether she would be happier living somewhere else.

Feeling rejected and despondent, Gina went to her room and wrote a note saying that she was having a mental breakdown and that she loved her parents but could not communicate with them. She added a request that her favorite glass animals be given to a particular friend. Her parents, who had gone out to see a movie, returned home later that evening to find their daughter comatose and immediately rushed her to the hospital emergency room.

Over the previous few months, Gina had been crying frequently and had lost interest in her friends, school, and social activities. She was eating more and more and had recently begun to gain weight, which made her mother very unhappy. Gina said that her mother was always harping about Gina's "taking care of herself." In fact, the argument on the night of Gina's suicide attempt was about Gina's desire to order a pizza that her mother did not think she needed. Gina's mother reported that all her daughter seemed to want to do was sleep and that she never wanted to go out with her friends or help around the house. When questioned about changes in her sleep habits, Gina admitted that she had been feeling very tired and that she often felt as if there was nothing in her life that made it worth getting out of bed. She mentioned that she was excited about an upcoming visit from her boyfriend, who attended a faraway college and had not been home for several months.

Upon evaluation, it became apparent that this teenager, the third of three children born to upper-middle-class and highly intelligent parents, was struggling with a view of herself as less bright, clever, and attractive than her two siblings. She felt ignored and rejected by her hardworking father and in hostile conflict with her well-organized mother. Gina was having trouble developing a sense of separation from her mother and an image of her own unique identity. She experienced her mother's directives as interference with her personal efforts to express autonomy and independence.

Gina was kept overnight in the hospital in an adolescent psychiatric unit and seen by a female psychiatrist who was able to connect with her. She was prescribed an antidepressant specially selected so it would not cause her to gain weight, since her depression had already led her to put on weight. Her doctor stated that Gina would likely only have to take medication for a short period of time. What Gina really needed for long-term improvement was family therapy with her mother and father, as well as her siblings, present (Figure 2.1).[2]

Symptoms of Major Depressive Disorder

Gina is experiencing major depressive disorder. She has the combination and duration of symptoms, as well as an impairment of functioning as a result of her symptoms. It appears that

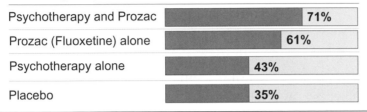

Talk and pills help adolescent depression

Psychotherapy and Prozac together work better than either method alone in treating depression in adolescents, including reducing suicidal thoughts, a new study found.

Percentage of patients showing improvement

Psychotherapy and Prozac	71%
Prozac (Fluoxetine) alone	61%
Psychotherapy alone	43%
Placebo	35%

SOURCE: Journal of the American Medical Association   AP

Figure 2.1 Adolescent depression is best treated with a combination of psychotherapy and drug therapy. Patients have shown a 71% improvement rate using both methods of treatment.

the intense stress of dealing with her family dynamics has led to this depressive episode for Gina, although there are likely other factors that also played a role. In an unfortunate cycle of events, Gina's depression caused weight gain, leading her mother to make comments about her appetite and appearance, which further aggravated Gina's depression.

People with major depressive disorder can develop a pessimistic and negative view of themselves and the world around them. Their self-esteem plummets and they tend to blame themselves for things that may not have anything to do with them. They might have suicidal thoughts, along with the mistaken belief that no one would miss them if they were gone or that others might even be happier if they died. This is part of the disease of depression. Major depressive disorder can become so severe that it causes a person to exhibit unusual or bizarre thoughts or perceptions. The term *psychosis* is used in psychiatry to define symptoms that indicate a state of mind that is out of touch with reality. All of the mood disorders can sometimes occur with **psychotic features,** and when they do show up, these features are often severe. The most common psychotic symptoms are delusions and hallucinations.

Delusions are firmly fixed, false beliefs that are outside of the cultural norm. By definition, these beliefs are so strongly held that the person who holds them cannot be convinced that he or she is wrong. A psychotic individual may believe that he or she is evil and is being punished by God (this typically occurs during a major depressive episode). People in psychotic states may also become very paranoid, to the point that they believe family members are plotting to hurt them.

Hallucinations are sensory experiences that occur in the absence of sensory stimulation. They can involve any of the five senses. The most common ones seen with mood disorders are auditory hallucinations, such as hearing voices. The voices may just be mumbling or they may say things that are insulting to the affected person. A milder form of hallucinations includes hearing noises such as a radio, static, or a telephone, or hearing one's name being called. Occasionally, a person will have a visual hallucination such as seeing the visual image of a deceased person or an apparition.

The presence of psychotic symptoms makes the process of diagnosing mood disorders more difficult. The DSM-IV defines an entire category of psychotic disorders that consist of illnesses such as schizophrenia, **schizoaffective disorder, delusional disorder,** and **brief psychotic disorder.** Therefore, it can often be difficult to tell which illness is occurring—a mood disorder or a psychotic disorder. The treatment and **prognosis** can be very different for each.

Major Depressive Disorder with Psychotic Features

During her initial psychiatric evaluation, Clara, a 38-year-old mother of three, had a look of dread on her face. Her hands picked restlessly at the sores on her arms. For several weeks before this consultation, she had become more and more withdrawn, and during the interview, she responded only with grunts and nods. Clara's husband, who accompanied her to the visit, was extremely alarmed by his wife's symptoms. He reported that she said she was hearing voices that kept her from communicating with "outsiders." According to Clara, her mother, who had been dead for five years, was insisting that Clara kill herself so that they could be reunited. Her father was also appearing in both visual and auditory hallucinations. In addition, a medley of unrecognizable and tormenting voices were mocking Clara, and she told her husband that she could only silence the voices by banging her head sharply against the wall, although she usually didn't have enough energy to do this. Clara also believed that she had cancer and that her children were gravely ill.

This episode of depression began with a feeling of despair and emptiness. At night, Clara could not fall asleep because of the painful, recurring belief that she was a damaged creature. She blamed herself for her mother's death and felt that she was a witch who deserved to be burned. After waking up early each morning, she would sit shivering on the bathroom floor so that she would not disturb her husband. She wished that she had the will and courage to kill herself. Clara felt so hopeless and full of despair that she became convinced that nuclear war would soon end all life on the planet. She sat very still and looked like a lifeless shell of a person.

Clara had been hospitalized five times over the previous nine years. One hospitalization six years ago was characterized by symptoms very much like her current ones. Her other hospitalizations occurred due to severe depression and suicidal thoughts, but she had never shown psychotic symptoms before now. Her previous treatments included **electroconvulsive therapy** (**ECT**), antidepressants, and antipsychotic medication. Clara generally improved during her hospitalizations and was able to return home within six to eight weeks.

Clara did not function very well between her episodes, and her functioning before her first episode was also poor. There were only brief periods—days or occasionally weeks—when she found life worth living and felt that she could approach her responsibilities with reasonable energy and confidence. For the most part, she was a withdrawn and despairing per-

Did you know?
Ernest Hemingway

Ernest Hemingway suffered from major depressive disorder and died as a result of it. Ernest Hemingway was one of America's greatest writers. He authored such classics as *The Sun Also Rises*, *For Whom the Bell Tolls*, and *The Old Man and the Sea*. His novels are a staple in high school and college English classes to this day. In the latter part of his life, Hemingway battled with severe depression, alcoholism, and suicidal thoughts. He had received inpatient psychiatric treatment and even electroconvulsive therapy. Nonetheless, Hemingway lost his battle with his mood disorder—he committed suicide in July 1961. Interestingly, four of Hemingway's family members have committed suicide as well. They include his sister, brother, father, and granddaughter Margaux, who committed suicide in 1996.

Known Sufferers of Major Depressive Disorder

- Drew Carey, actor and comedian
- Mike Wallace, CBS news host of *60 Minutes*
- Tom Johnson, former president of CNN (Cable News Network)
- Shawn Colvin, singer/ songwriter
- Sheryl Crow, singer/ songwriter
- Lorraine Bracco, actress
- Olympia Dukakis, actress
- Harrison Ford, actor
- Elton John, musician
- Barbara Bush, former U.S. first lady
- George Stephanopoulis, advisor to President Bill Clinton and ABC news host
- Tipper Gore, wife of former U.S vice president Al Gore
- Ashley Judd, actress
- Anthony Hopkins, actor

son who spent many hours alone, feeling empty and sad. Because she only occasionally felt up to preparing meals or shopping, her husband hired a housekeeper to run the house and care for the kids. Clara had only one friend, whom she rarely saw. She loved her children but also avoided them. Close contact with them often infuriated her, and she worried about being a bad mother.[3]

SYMPTOMS OF MAJOR DEPRESSIVE DISORDER WITH PSYCHOTIC FEATURES

Major depressive disorder with psychotic features is one of the most severe mood disorders. It can be catastrophically disabling for the affected person and devastating for his or her family. Sufferers experience both impaired functioning in their daily lives and a large number of symptoms that last for long periods of time. How severe this depression is can be seen in the fact that Clara grunts instead of using normal speech, and that she also suffers from auditory hallucinations and delusions (about nuclear war and the illnesses she believes she and her family suffer from), making this a psychotic mood disorder. Clara's illness is so severe that both her safety and that of her children is in question. Major depressive disorder with psychotic features requires urgent intervention and, in many cases, hospitalization is necessary.

3

The Bipolar Spectrum Disorders

The bipolar spectrum disorders are mood disorders that occur with some regularity throughout the world. **Bipolar I disorder** occurs in about 1–2% of the population, independent of gender. These disorders cause any elevation in mood, such as a manic or **hypomanic episode**. The term *bipolarity* refers to severe mood swings over weeks or months that go from an extreme of euphoria or irritability to depression (Figure 3.1). An older term for the bipolar spectrum disorders, and especially for bipolar disorder type I, is **manic depression**. This name is still used today, although it is not found in DSM-IV. There are three types of bipolar disorder: type I, which is the most severe; type II, which is less severe; and **cyclothymic disorder**, which is the mildest form.

MANIC EPISODES

At the heart of the bipolar spectrum of disorders is the **manic episode.** If you think of the human brain as an engine, mania is as if someone stepped on the accelerator. A manic episode is an expansive or elevated mood state that includes very rapid thoughts, loads of energy without the need to sleep, talkativeness, and overflowing self-esteem and **grandiose** thinking, sometimes to the point of losing touch with reality. People in a severe manic episode may be bouncing off the walls ·and claiming to be royalty or to have friends or acquaintances in

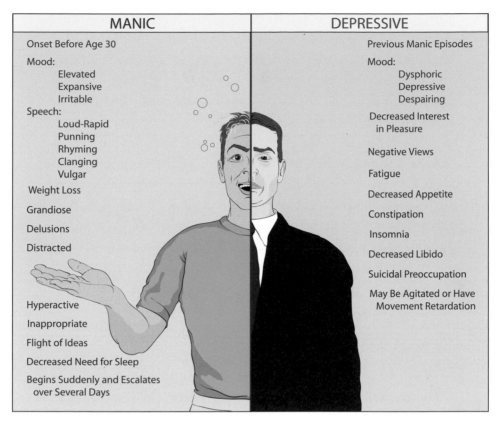

MANIC	DEPRESSIVE
Onset Before Age 30	Previous Manic Episodes

Mood:
    Elevated
    Expansive
    Irritable
	Mood:
	    Dysphoric
	    Depressive
	    Despairing

Speech:
    Loud-Rapid
    Punning
    Rhyming
    Clanging
    Vulgar
	Decreased Interest
	    in Pleasure

	Negative Views
Weight Loss	Fatigue
Grandiose	Decreased Appetite
Delusions	Constipation
Distracted	Insomnia
	Decreased Libido
	Suicidal Preoccupation
Hyperactive	May Be Agitated or Have Movement Retardation
Inappropriate	
Flight of Ideas	
Decreased Need for Sleep	
Begins Suddenly and Escalates over Several Days	

Figure 3.1 People with bipolar disorder experience extreme emotions. The manic stage, also called a hypomanic episode, causes a person to feel elated or irritable and to act distracted or hyperactive. The depressive stage has the opposite effect, causing a person to feel an intense low and to lose interest in normal activities.

very high places. They may believe they can solve some of the greatest dilemmas of history in the fields of science, politics, religion, or the arts. They have rapid thoughts, so that they might be described as flighty and easily distracted. Manic people can be immensely productive if they can focus their energies on constructive tasks, but they can also get agitated if things slow them down. They may become impulsive in various ways, such as seeking pleasure without regard to risks (in the form of drugs, sex, speeding while driving, or spending too much money). They may also feel that no one understands them and that the world is too slow or inferior to handle someone of their intellect and stature. Irritability can also be a major factor in mania. The irritability of a manic episode can make the mind and body grow weary of the pace. Irritability in the context of mania or hypomania can manifest in an aggressive and sometimes dangerous fashion. Individuals may shout, argue, experience road rage, kick a door, bang on a wall, throw things, or become violent with people. It also puts a manic individual at a much higher risk of suicide as a means to relieve the grueling irritability. A person exhibiting mania usually stands out from a crowd because his or her symptoms are disruptive to the environment. These symptoms have to persist for at least a week to qualify as mania.

Normal Versus Abnormal Moods

Example of normal mood state:

Elation felt for several hours or even days in response to great news, such as getting a highly sought-after college acceptance or getting a date to a school dance. Sleep cycle, appetite, and realistic decision making are all within normal range.

Example of an abnormal mood state, consistent with a bipolar spectrum disorder:

Boundless elation, whether spontaneous or out of proportion to its trigger, such that it is uncharacteristic or unusual. In addition, the person might feel "wired" all day and night, sleeping less than three hours per night and making grandiose, unrealistic plans.

Psychotic symptoms such as delusions and/or hallucinations can also occur with severe bipolar disorder. Most people with mania need medical treatment in a psychiatric hospital.

MIXED EPISODES

One mood episode we have not yet examined is the **mixed episode**. A mixed episode involves symptoms of both mania and depression. Imagine being "wired" with tons of restless energy and racing thoughts, while at the same time feeling sad, tearful, and intensely depressed. It's as if the accelerator and brakes are pushed simultaneously—something is bound to break. A mixed episode can be very dangerous, because it may lead to a suicide attempt. These attempts are not only due to the sadness, but are also a result of agitation that may make a person stop at nothing to find relief, even if that means suicide. Mixed episodes are usually medical emergencies.

CASE STUDY 1

Bipolar Disorder, Type I with Psychotic Features
Anna, a 30-year-old schoolteacher, was dragged to the hospital by her parents, each pulling one of her arms. When the clinician entered the consultation room, Anna was pacing restlessly and singing "The Battle Hymn of the Republic." When introduced to the doctor, Anna noticed his green tie and assumed that his name was Dr. Green. She consoled him for having brown eyes rather than green, but assured him that he could change his eye color if he only wished hard enough. Her attention immediately switched to something else, and Anna covered eight different topics in the first two minutes of her meeting with the doctor.

Although Anna was at first friendly and flirtatious, offering to show the doctor a bruise on her upper thigh, when the clinician suggested hospitalization, she became furious and threatened to hit him. She screamed that her parents had bribed him to put her in the hospital so they could collect her disability insurance. She shouted that she had friends in the Mafia whom she would instruct to wipe out both the doctor and her parents.

This episode began suddenly ten days earlier, shortly after Anna broke up with her most recent boyfriend. Since that time, she had been sleeping only a few hours a night, had lost eight pounds, had ordered several thousand dollars' worth of special textbooks for her students, and had made dozens of long-distance calls. At the time of her initial evaluation, Anna was actually booked on a flight to the West Coast that was scheduled to depart in a few hours.

Anna had been hearing voices, both male and female, which told her that she was the princess of a small European country and had been smuggled into the United States at birth by her parents, who were imposters. She believed the voices were inspired by her real, royal parents but said she did not know who they were or how they transmitted their voices. She also believed that her thoughts could influence the course of future events and that her dreams were appearing in a disguised form in the daily newspaper.

Anna's thought patterns were described in the doctor's note as "racing and disconnected." Her speech was described as "pressured and occasionally hard to comprehend."

Anna has had three previous episodes during the past two years, each of which began in a similar manner and then progressed to a major depressive episode that lasted four to eight weeks. Between episodes, Anna was not delusional or hallucinating, and her thoughts were not disordered. Although she had experimented with drugs and alcohol in the past, she had not used any drug within the last three years. Despite all her problems, Anna was a relatively steady worker, supported herself, and was able to live alone.

Anna was diagnosed as having an acute manic episode as a result of her recurrent bipolar disorder, type I. She was ordered to undergo inpatient psychiatric treatment against her wishes because both a physician and a clinical psychologist determined that she was suffering from a severe mood disorder that was impairing her judgment, her safety, and her ability to care for herself. Anna was still furious about the admission and required an injection of a sedative medication to allow medical personnel to transfer her to the locked psychiatric unit. In the psychiatric unit, Anna received injectable medications because she refused to take medication by mouth, denying that she had any problem that needed treatment. After several doses of medication, Anna slept for several hours and the nurses noted that when she woke up, she was a little less "hyper." By the third day in the hospital, Anna had agreed to take her medication orally, was sleeping better, and admitted to having felt "a little wired" before coming to the hospital.

On her eighth day of hospitalization, Anna was a changed person. She was calm, polite, and cooperative. She acknowledged the fact that she had a major psychiatric illness that needed treatment. She also attended group therapy with other patients and even contributed by talking about her history with bipolar disorder. Her psychiatrist and other staff members determined that she could be discharged and have follow-up treatment as an outpatient. She was given appointments for both a psychiatrist and a psychologist as part of her aftercare and was told about a weekly bipolar disorder support group in her area.

Anna had used nine days of sick leave from her job but returned to work without any problem. A month later, doctors noted that she was taking her medication and attending weekly

psychotherapy sessions, and that her symptoms were still under control. One thing Anna did not like was that her medication (Depakote®) caused her to gain weight. She mentioned this to her therapist, who notified her psychiatrist, indicating that it may be a risk for her stopping the medication on her own. Anna's psychiatrist addressed this at their next meeting, and they have developed several strategies to combat this side effect before they decide to change medication.[4]

SYMPTOMS OF BIPOLAR DISORDER TYPE I

Anna's case illustrates a severe case of bipolar disorder. What is described is a manic episode with many of the features of the condition, including hyperactivity, pressured speech, decreased need for sleep, and racing thoughts. Anna is irritable and impulsive (she threatens to hit the doctor and spends excessive amounts of money), and psychotic (she hears multiple voices and believes that she is a princess).

Anna's case provides a good example of just how severe bipolar disorder can be. One must remember that these disorders involve significant shifts in mood (Figure 3.2). These are *not* the mood shifts that most people have in everyday life. The common denominator to the diagnosis of these disorders is that they must cause a certain level of symptoms, for a certain duration of time, causing a certain level of social or occupational dysfunction. If these three conditions are met, a diagnosis can be made and treatment is usually warranted.

CASE STUDY 2

Bipolar Disorder Type II

Mr. Z was a 45-year-old married business administrator who was admitted to a psychiatric unit at a teaching hospital for

Manic and Depressive Episodes

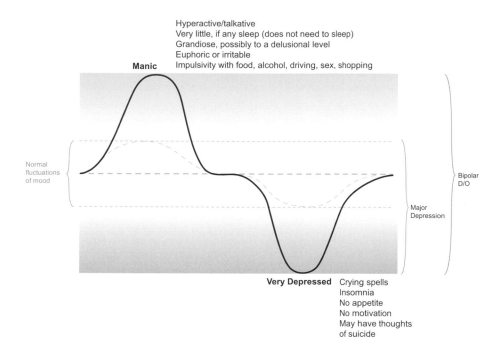

Figure 3.2 Significant shift in mood is a symptom of severe bipolar disorder. During a hypomanic episode, mood fluctuates to an abnormally high level that causes feelings of euphoria, grandiose, or irritability. On the opposite side of the spectrum, major depressive episodes cause crying spells, insomnia, and possibly suicidal thoughts.

evaluation. He had had two psychiatric hospitalizations previously for depression and suicidal thoughts during the preceding two years. At the time of this admission, as in his earlier admissions, he denied having any psychiatric illness. During the two weeks before he was admitted, Mr. Z spent most of his time lying in bed (claiming this was due to physical illness) and refused to go to work or take part in his family's life in any way. His wife reported that his mood had been persistently gloomy and pessimistic and that he had

Did you know? Jane Pauley has been diagnosed with bipolar disorder.

Jane Pauley is a longtime television news reporter. From 1976 to 1989, she was cohost of NBC's *The Today Show*. Then, from 1992 to 2003, she was a cohost of NBC's *Dateline*. Pauley revealed the fact that she suffered from bipolar disorder in a candid autobiography published in 2004, entitled *Skywriting: A Life Out of the Blue*.

Jane Pauley's episodes of major depression and mania began in 1999, after she received steroid treatment for a skin condition. This treatment was thought to trigger an underlying predilection she had for a mood disorder. She has stated that her late father may have had bipolar disorder that went undiagnosed. Pauley's bout with this disease played a role in her decision to leave her job at *Dateline*. In her book, she explains that during one of her manic phases, she impulsively bought a house over the Internet. She reports that she underwent treatment at a psychiatric hospital and was even on suicide watch. The central factors in her recovery have been the support of her family, understanding her disease, and treatment with the medication lithium.

frequently become irritable with her when she suggested possible courses of action that might help him.

According to his wife, throughout their marriage, Mr. Z had often experienced periods of dejection and depression in which he seemed to have a hard time doing anything. She also reported, however, that he had sudden bursts of excessive energy that usually lasted from a few days to several weeks. During his energetic periods, he stayed late at work, often keeping several secretaries busy with his productivity. He also plunged into volunteer activities—most recently, writing speeches for local politicians—and designed and began elaborate exercise programs. During some of these episodes, Mr. Z suddenly announced that he had planned an exotic and elaborate family vacation for which they were expected to leave almost immediately. Although his wife and daughter usually agreed to accompany him on these jaunts, he vacationed at such a vigorous pace—mountain climbing in Europe or scuba diving in the Caribbean—that his family struggled unsuccessfully to keep up with him. It was after returning from one of these whirlwind vacations that Mr. Z impulsively bought an expensive piece of land because it was similar to an Australian farm he had admired. Mr. Z's wife estimated that he experienced five or six hypomanic episodes each year, each lasting between three days and two weeks. She also reported that this pattern of behavior was already established when she first met Mr. Z in college. He did fairly well in school but would fluctuate between irritable "glum" periods when he would sleep late and miss classes, and marathon two- or three-day study binges.

Mr. Z's wife said that his brief bursts of energy tended to vanish as suddenly as they came and that Mr. Z then let his projects lapse, often becoming gloomy and pessimistic about them. Beginning when he was 32 years old, Mr. Z had been treated on four occasions for major depressive episodes, each of which lasted approximately four to five months. He was hospitalized for two of these episodes in the past two years, on one occasion following a serious car accident that was judged to be a suicide attempt, although he denied this.

His wife reported that his severe depressions had always occurred in the fall and winter, whereas his energetic periods had been especially common in spring and summer. She said that she had come to dread the winter, which she associated with the possibility that her husband would have yet another depressive episode.

When questioned about his energetic periods, Mr. Z said that, although he realized he sometimes went too far and lost control, he preferred these times because he felt so intensely alive, had so much fun, and accomplished so much. He said he could remember having such brief bursts of productivity since he was in his early teens or even earlier, and that he had always been a flighty person whose moods changed quickly.[5]

SYMPTOMS OF BIPOLAR DISORDER TYPE II

Bipolar II disorder is similar to bipolar I except that instead of a manic episode, it involves a hypomanic episode and a major depressive episode. *Hypomania* is the term used to describe a milder version of mania. The symptoms can be very similar to those seen in mania but are less severe and last for a shorter period of time (as little as a few days). People who experience hypomania may go undiagnosed and may just be described as "hyper" or revved up. They may get a lot done, sleep very little, and actually look forward to periods when they are more productive and feel great.

As illustrated by this case, although Mr. Z has a diagnosis of bipolar disorder type II, he is currently being treated for a major depressive episode. The treatment differs for the depressive episodes of bipolar disorder compared to those of major depressive disorder. Another good feature of this case is how it illustrates hypomania. Mr. Z's elevated mood episodes are never so severe as to cause delusional thinking or behavior that puts him or others in harm's way.

Why is there no mood disorder that involves only hypomania? As you can see, the diagnosis of bipolar disorder type II requires both a major depressive episode and hypomania. Hypomania by itself may not be an "abnormal" mood state. There are plenty of people who are bright, energetic, and happy all the time, and may even get by on less than a full eight hours of sleep per night. Do they suffer from a mood disorder? Probably not. The diagnosis of a mood disorder requires that the mood symptoms cause some sort of disruption to the activities

Known Sufferers of Bipolar Disorder

- Ted Turner, founder of cable channels CNN and TBS (whose father committed suicide)
- Tim Burton, film director
- Buzz Aldrin, astronaut
- Patty Duke, actress
- Carrie Fisher, actress and author
- Linda Hamilton, actress
- Kitty Dukakis, former first lady of Massachusetts
- Francis Ford Coppola, film director
- Axl Rose, rock singer
- Jean-Claude Van Damme, actor

of life. A "hypomanic personality" may not necessarily cause any dysfunction by itself—it may, in fact, prove to be somewhat beneficial. This is why a major depressive episode combined with hypomania creates a special kind of mood disorder, known as bipolar disorder type II. The major depressive symptoms usually give rise to the dysfunction (thereby leading to the diagnosis of a mood disorder) and the hypomania places the disorder within the bipolar spectrum.

Cyclothymic Disorder

Mr. F, a 27-year-old single man, came for a psychiatric evaluation at the insistence of his girlfriend because he had been irritable, jumpy, excessively energetic, unable to sleep, and dissatisfied with the humdrum nature of his work and life. He had many such episodes that usually lasted for a few days but sometimes lasted as long as a few weeks and usually alternated with slightly longer periods (weeks to months) of feeling dejected, hopeless, worn out, and wanting to die. He described himself as an "emotional roller coaster" and said that his moods might shift as many as 20 to 30 times in a year. Mr. F reported that he had been this way for as long as he could remember. He had never been treated for this behavior, despite two impulsive suicide attempts with alcohol and sleeping pills. However, his symptoms had never met the full criteria for either a major depressive episode or a manic episode, nor had he ever had symptoms of psychosis or severe depression. Mr. F denied using drugs and claimed that he drank alcohol only occasionally to relax.

Mr. F had a chaotic life. He was brought up by a succession of aunts and uncles, none of whom had been very pleased with the task. He was an irresponsible, trouble-making child, frequently running away, being absent from school, and com-

Cyclothymic Disorder

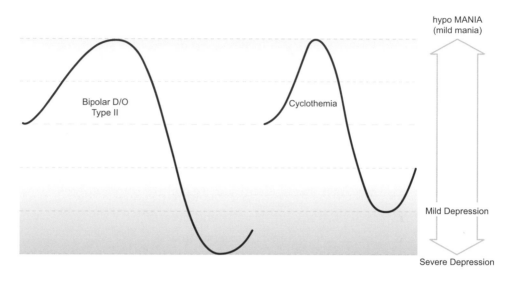

Figure 3.3 Cyclothymic disorder is a milder version of a bipolar spectrum disorder. Elevations and depressions in mood are less dramatic and thus do not meet the criteria for hypomanic or major depressive episodes.

mitting small thefts. At the age of 16, Mr. F hitched a ride to a distant city and never returned or called home. Since that time, he had drifted around the country, working irregularly as a car washer or night watchman, on a road construction crew, and at other unskilled jobs. He would get restless and then move on to other jobs. He formed friendships quickly but then gave them up just as fast.[6]

This case sounds like it could be any of the bipolar spectrum disorders. It nicely illustrates how complicated the process of diagnosing a mood disorder can be. In cases like this, it is very important to obtain information from a variety of sources such as schoolteachers, former and current bosses, girlfriends or boyfriends, and family members.

SYMPTOMS OF CYCLOTHYMIC DISORDER
Cyclothymic disorder is a milder version of a bipolar spectrum disorder that consists of clinical elevations and depressions in mood that do not meet the criteria for hypomanic or major depressive episodes (Figure 3.3).

CHILDHOOD BIPOLAR DISORDER
Although most cases of bipolar disorder first occur in early adulthood, they have been identified in children and adolescents as well. Symptoms similar to those explained above for adults can occur in young people, but there may also be other age-specific symptoms, such as temper tantrums, yelling, and defiance of authority. A child who is manic may engage in daredevil behaviors or have extreme and rapid mood swings. Bipolar disorder that develops in childhood is often difficult to distinguish from **attention-deficit/hyperactivity disorder** (**ADHD**).

MANIC DISORDER?
You may notice from the above descriptions that there is no mood disorder that consists solely of mania. With our current level of understanding, an individual with a history of just one manic episode is still diagnosed with bipolar disorder, even if he or she has never had a major depressive episode. It is believed that the major depressive episode will eventually occur at a later time, although some patients may never experience a major depressive disorder. This is very uncommon, however.

Other Mood Disorders

Two unique mood disorders exist that involve either a major depressive disorder or the depressed phase of bipolar disorder. These are **postpartum depression** and **seasonal affective disorder** (**SAD**).

POSTPARTUM DEPRESSION

In 2005, Brooke Shields, the well-known actress and model, revealed that after the birth of her daughter, she sank into a severe depression that would not end. She sought treatment with medication and psychotherapy and wrote a book about her experience entitled *Down Came the Rain* (Figure 4.1).

Postpartum depression is a unique mood disorder that afflicts women after childbirth. The symptoms are the same as major depressive disorder, but the difference is that they occur soon after childbirth. The risk of suffering from postpartum depression among all women from one month to a year after childbirth is 10%. The risk is close to 50% for women who have a prior history of postpartum depression. The cause of this increased risk has been shown to be the drastic change of hormone levels that occurs immediately after childbirth, including **estradiol**, **progesterone**, and **androgens**. The "**postpartum blues**" are considered a normal emotional response after the birth of a child, not a disease. Postpartum depression is much worse and more persistent, usually requiring professional treatment

Figure 4.1 Brooke Shields shared her battle with postpartum depression in her book, *Down Came the Rain*.

(Figure 4.2). Other possible postpartum psychiatric reactions include mania and psychosis, although these are less common.

Figure 4.2 Postpartum depression requires professional treatment. Organizations such as New Jersey Speak Up offer resources for mothers and families affected by postpartum depression.

SEASONAL AFFECTIVE DISORDER

This condition, also known as major depressive disorder (or bipolar disorder) with seasonal pattern, is a mood disorder where a major depressive episode occurs regularly at a particular time of year, usually winter, and goes away at a different time of year, usually spring. This type of mood disorder is unique in that it can sometimes be treated using **light therapy**.

MOOD DISORDERS DUE TO OTHER CAUSES

There are two types of mood disorders that must be distinguished from all of those we have discussed thus far. They consist of symptoms that can exactly mimic a depressive disorder or a bipolar spectrum disorder, but they are brought on by either a medical illness or a substance such as a medication, toxin, drug, or alcohol. Often, there is no difference in the way these disorders look—they can perfectly mimic bipolar disorder or a major depressive disorder. A detailed history and record review by a medical professional, however, can often reveal one of these conditions.

A **mood disorder due to general medical condition** is diagnosed when symptoms of a mood disorder (either manic or depressive) exist but can be attributed to the biological effects of a disease affecting the brain. Note that this is not an emotional reaction to having the disease, but a physiological effect. Examples

Substances That Can Cause a Mood Disorder

Prescription Drugs

- Amphetamines or stimulants like Ritalin®
- Opiates (for pain)
- Antihypertensives (for treatment of high blood pressure)
- Corticosteroids (hormones that, when used as drugs, reduce swelling and decrease the immune response)
- Immunosuppressants (drugs that reduce the immune response)
- Antibiotics (drugs that kill bacteria)
- Beta-blockers (drugs that affect the body's response to nerve impulses)

Drugs of Abuse:

- Cocaine
- Heroin
- Alcohol
- LSD
- PCP
- Ecstasy (MDMA)
- Marijuana

include thyroid dysfunction, stroke, brain tumor, HIV/AIDS, or multiple sclerosis (MS).

A **substance-induced mood disorder** is a condition (either manic or depressive) caused by the biological effects of foreign substances, such as medications, illicit drugs, or ingested toxins. Examples of recreational or illicit drugs include alcohol, marijuana, cocaine, stimulants, anabolic steroids, and virtually any mood-altering substance. Certain prescription drugs, such as blood pressure medications, antibiotics, or prescription steroids like prednisone, may also cause mood symptoms. Finally, toxins such as lead or mercury can produce psychiatric effects because they affect the brain.

There are two separate disorders that cause symptoms similar to those seen with the mood disorders. They are classified differently as the adjustment disorders and bereavement. An **adjustment disorder** can involve depressive symptoms and occurs in direct response to a new stressor. Most people react to new stressors, but to have an adjustment disorder, a person's symptoms must interfere with daily functioning. **Bereavement** is a normal human experience—the natural response to the death of a loved one, whether it be a family member, friend, or pet. Treatment is usually not necessary, although some people may seek it. The existence of excessive guilt or thoughts of death or suicide is usually considered an abnormal grief reaction and may require treatment.

CASE STUDY 1

Mood Disorder Due to General Medical Condition (Hypothyroidism)
Mrs. J, a 65-year-old widow of two years, visited her medical doctor because of increasing fatigue, lethargy, and depression that had developed over the past six months. Her symptoms began gradually, but over the past month, they worsened to

the point that she was having trouble getting out of bed in the morning, quit her volunteer job at the local hospital, and stopped a number of her usual social activities at church. She did not seem to have any motivation, and it had become difficult to perform even the most basic activities of daily living, such as cooking and housekeeping. Mrs. J reported that she had been sleeping too much (sometimes 10–12 hours per day) and had gained weight (15 pounds over the past month) because of her inactivity. She also complained of aches and pains, difficulty staying warm, and a range of other physical discomforts. Other family members had recently remarked about how tired she looked. Mrs. J's daughter was very concerned because her mother had dropped out of so many activities that she used to enjoy and did not even show much interest in spending time with her two young grandchildren, to whom she had always been devoted. Mrs. J reported that she was frequently tearful and was beginning to feel like a burden on the daughter with whom she lived. Most of the household chores that she used to help with now fell to her daughter, who also cared for two small children, and her husband. Mrs. J said she had started to wonder whether she wouldn't be better off dead, so that "I would not be a burden on everyone." Mrs. J reported that her concentration had declined over the past few months, that she frequently misplaced things, and that she even had trouble following the plot of television programs. She denied experiencing any delusions or hallucinations.

Mrs. J had no history of depression, excessive alcohol use, or problems with memory before six months ago. She had never been hospitalized for psychiatric problems, nor was there any family history of such problems.

When she had a physical exam by a doctor, Mrs. J had a normal temperature with a slightly low pulse of 55 (normal is

60–100), a normal blood pressure of 120/80, and respirations of 14 per minute. Her face appeared a bit swollen and there was swelling in her legs. Her neurological exam was normal, and her reflexes were symmetrical but slowed. The rest of the physical exam was normal.

Her doctor did a screening for medical problems, including a blood count and thyroid test. Mrs. J's thyroid test revealed that she had too little thyroid hormone in her bloodstream. Mrs. J was placed on a dose of levothyroxine (a thyroid supplement) and, after one month of treatment, she began to notice her energy returning and felt a gradual improvement in her mood and outlook. She resumed her volunteer work at the hospital and her social activities at church. After three months of treatment, Mrs. J was back to her usual self. Two years later, Mrs. J had not experienced any recurrence of her symptoms.[7]

In this case, Mrs. J experienced many of the symptoms of major depressive disorder. In addition, however, she had some physical symptoms that indicated a thyroid disturbance: low pulse, slow reflexes, weight gain, and swelling of the extremities. All of her symptoms disappeared when her medical condition was treated with thyroid medication. It is often impossible to tell the difference between major depressive disorder and a case like this. A physical exam and laboratory tests are necessary.

There are many known medical and neurological disorders that can cause a mood disorder. Illnesses that can produce symptoms of either depression, mania, or both include hypo- or hyperthyroidism, an excess or deficiency of the hormone **cortisol**, **epilepsy**, hydrocephalus (excess fluid in the brain), sleep apnea (a breathing disturbance during sleep), stroke, lupus, brain tumors, MS, or certain infections. Finally, anemia (low red

Did you know?
Steps for Diagnosing a Mood Disorder

There are a series of questions that must be answered before a mood disorder can be diagnosed. A diagnosis of a mood disorder can only be made by a qualified health-care professional. Here is a basic questionnaire that may be used as a starting point.

Are there mood symptoms present?

This question is fairly obvious—does the person show symptoms of a mood disorder?

Are the symptoms prominent and do they cause dysfunction?

One requirement for the diagnosis of a mood disorder is that the symptoms it causes must be severe enough to cause social, occupational, or educational dysfunction. To be diagnosed, an individual's ability to function is hampered to the point that he or she is being admonished at work or school for poor performance, is taking personal/sick days because of the mood disorder, or has been suspended or dismissed.

Are the symptoms caused by a general medical condition or due to the direct effect of a substance?

This is an important question to answer because, if the answer is yes, then it is nearly impossible to diagnose mood disorders such as bipolar disorder or major depressive disorder. The diagnosis is either mood disorder due to general medical condition or substance-induced mood disorder. The treatment strategy is vastly different for these conditions because one would want to treat the underlying medical condition or eliminate the action of the substance in question in order to treat the mood symptoms.

Is there a different psychiatric disorder present?

The one category of disorders that must be ruled out is schizophrenia and other psychotic disorders. A person with a mood disorder may have psychotic symptoms, but thought must be given to the possibility that a distinct psychotic disorder exists. One of the reasons for this is that the treatment of psychotic disorders is very different from the treatment for mood disorders.

Are there symptoms of mania, hypomania, or a mixed episode?

If the answer is yes, a detailed history must be taken to determine whether any current or former symptoms meet the criteria for one of these three episodes. If so, this would lead to a diagnosis of one of the bipolar spectrum disorders.

If the symptoms do not meet the criteria for mania, hypomania, or a mixed episode, then one of the depressive disorders may be diagnosed.

The information required to make a diagnosis of a mood disorder may be obtained from the individual or, with the person's permission, from his or her friends or family members, or from outside sources such as medical records or police reports.

blood cell count) and vitamin deficiencies can also cause a mood disturbance, usually depression.

CASE STUDY 2

Substance-Induced Mood Disorder (From Alcohol)

Ms. R was a 40-year-old married businesswoman with four children. She was admitted to a hospital for treatment of her alcoholism at the insistence of her family. She had been drinking a quart of gin a day and was having frequent severe fights with her husband. She had been waking up very early in the morning and would lie "there thinking about how everyone would be better off if I were dead." She had always prided herself on being well groomed and nicely dressed, but lately she had felt too tired and demoralized to care what she wore or how she looked. Her family reported that she would burst into tears when confronted with the most minor problems or criticism.

Ms. R's heavy drinking began 10 years ago, soon after she discovered that her husband was having an affair. She said that ever since she discovered his disloyalty, her predominant feeling for her husband had been contempt. Nevertheless, she felt unable to leave the marriage because she and her husband were business partners and she continued to feel dependent on him to make certain decisions and handle aspects of the business that had always been his responsibility. Although Ms. R's capabilities made her indispensable, she often missed work, made major errors in judgment, and caused scenes. Her daughter complained that her mother's behavior had become embarrassing to the entire family.

During the past two years, she began drinking in the morning and experienced periods of memory loss. On one occasion, she was arrested for driving while intoxicated. She denied using substances other than alcohol.

Ms. R expressed a wish to die but said she did not have "the courage to commit suicide." Although she was embarrassed to need help, she had tried and failed many times to stop drinking, both on her own and with her doctor's help. She began to cry several times during the interview and repeatedly described herself as being a burden on everyone.

A year ago, Ms. R spent a month in an alcohol treatment program, where she appeared to make rapid progress through counseling and participation in Alcoholics Anonymous (AA). Her family reported that as soon as Ms. R recovered from the acute effects of alcohol withdrawal, her mood improved and she began to show a much brighter outlook and to make optimistic plans for the future. She planned to stop drinking, to continue in AA, to reduce her involvement with the business, and to consider marital counseling or, if that was not successful, to separate from her husband. Unfortunately, within two months, Ms. R had fallen back into her usual pattern. She resumed a full workload, stopped attending AA meetings, began battling with her husband, and started drinking heavily again. Her depressive symptoms returned and intensified, and, over the past 10 months, she experienced increasing hopelessness, inability to concentrate, and weight gain, as well as early morning awakening.

Ms. R. had a strong family history of alcoholism, including an alcoholic father who was violent with her mother. Throughout her childhood, she felt embarrassed and humiliated by her father, whom she both loved and despised. At the age of 16, she eloped with her present husband and soon became pregnant. Although he was abusive, she felt trapped in the marriage and proceeded to have three more children.[8]

By studying this case, we can see that Ms. R's depressive symptoms only occur while she is using alcohol and that her symptoms go away when she maintains sobriety, even if it is only for a short time. There are many prescription drugs and drugs of abuse that can cause either depression or mania. Ms. R's case is an example of alcohol causing a depressive disorder. Prescription drugs that may cause symptoms of a mood disorder include stimulants or amphetamines, opiates (for pain), blood pressure medications, corticosteroids, immunosuppressants, and even antibiotics.

Mood Disorders and Suicide

5

One of the main reasons to learn about mood disorders is because of their potential impact upon society. One such impact is felt through their death toll. The World Health Organization (WHO) states that suicide is among the top ten leading causes of death in every country in the world and estimates that there are nearly one million suicides annually around the globe.[9] Suicide has probably been around as long as humankind, but it has been misunderstood throughout much of history.

CAUSES OF SUICIDE

Twin studies, family studies, and adoption studies have all shown that there is a distinct genetic basis for suicide—that it is something more than a random choice.[10] Studies of the biology of suicide have found that depressed patients who attempt or complete suicide have a lower level of certain serotonin metabolites in their **cerebrospinal fluid**. This fluid is found in the spinal column up to the brain and is useful for studying metabolism in the central nervous system.

One common misconception about suicidal thinking is that it is somehow a moral flaw or a deficit in character. If life is compared to a game, then suicide is often equated with forfeiture. Another misperception is that suicidal thoughts can be

Did you know?

SUICIDE

- In the United States, approximately 30,000 individuals die by suicide each year.
- Suicide is the third leading cause of death in the 15–24 age group.
- Every year, there are 650,000 individuals brought to emergency rooms as a result of suicide attempts.
- The most common method of completed suicide is by the use of a firearm.
- Drug or alcohol intoxication is involved in one-third to one-half of all suicides.
- Females attempt suicide three times more often than males.
- Males successfully commit suicide four times more often than females.

Suicide Risk Factors

- Alcohol dependence
- Depression
- Single, widowed, or divorced
- Living alone
- Compromised physical health
- Owning a firearm
- History of previous attempts
- History of rage or violence
- Age over 45
- White or Native American heritage
- Unemployed, retired, or having financial difficulties
- Recent loss (e.g., of a job or close relationship)

Suicides Throughout History:

- Brutus, Roman politician, assassin of Julius Caesar, 42 B.C.
- Marc Antony, Roman politician and Cleopatra's lover, 30 B.C.
- Judas Iscariot, the apostle who betrayed Jesus, A.D. 33
- Robert Clive, British conqueror of India, 1774
- Thomas Jefferson Rusk, U.S. senator from Texas, 1857
- Vincent Van Gogh, Dutch painter and artist, 1890
- Barcroft Boake, Australian poet, 1892
- Virginia Woolf, British writer, 1941
- Edwin Howard Armstrong, pioneer of FM radio, 1954
- Getúlio Dornelles Vargas, former president of Brazil, 1954
- George Reeves, actor who played Superman on television, 1959
- Ernest Hemingway, American writer, 1961
- Sylvia Plath, American poet and author, 1963
- Dorothy Dandridge, African-American actress and singer, 1965
- Nick Drake, British folk singer, 1974
- Freddie Prinze, comedian and actor; father of Freddie Prinze, Jr., 1977
- Kurt Cobain, lead singer of Nirvana, 1994
- Vince Foster, White House lawyer for President Bill Clinton, 1993
- Margaux Hemingway, actress and model, 1996
- Dana Plato, actress from the TV show *Diff'rent Strokes*, 1999
- Hannelore Kohl, wife of former German chancellor Helmut Kohl, 2001
- Bernard Loiseau, French chef, 2003
- Spalding Gray, actor and writer, 2004
- Hunter S. Thompson, writer/journalist, 2005

normal, since it is natural for people to question their purpose in life and their place in this world. Although it may be normal to question life or wonder what death may be like, the presence of persistent suicidal thoughts is almost always an abnormal psychological state and is a medical emergency. Ninety percent of completed suicides occur in individuals who have a

Did you know?

Vincent Van Gogh

Vincent Van Gogh most likely suffered from bipolar I disorder. Vincent Van Gogh (see right) was a Dutch postimpressionist painter. Born in 1853, he lived to be only 37 years old, at which time he committed suicide. The year before his death, he wrote, "As for me, I am rather often uneasy in my mind, because I think that my life has not been calm enough; all those bitter disappointments, adversities, changes keep me from developing fully and naturally in my artistic career." In his youth, Van Gogh moved from job to job fairly regularly, often being dismissed—even from his schooling at an art academy. Van Gogh painted for only the last 10 years of his life and sold only one painting while he was alive. He suffered from many depressive episodes. He wrote, "when I am in the fields I am overwhelmed by a feeling of loneliness to such a horrible extent that I shy away from going out. . . ." In an infamous episode (possibly a manic state), he cut off part of his left ear and gave it to diagnosable (and usually treatable) psychiatric disorder at the time of death. About 60% of these people have a mood disorder.[11] Individuals experiencing suicidal thoughts need to be evaluated by a mental health professional immediately. This would involve obtaining a full psychiatric evaluation as well as an alcohol and drug use assessment. Treatment may involve

a female friend. Within the next year, he was admitted to a psychiatric facility, where he spent his time painting. The following year, in 1890, when he was beginning to receive critical acclaim for his work, Van Gogh fatally shot himself in the chest. His dying words, reported by his brother, were "*La tristesse durera toujours.*" ("The sadness will last forever.")

Dutch postimpressionist painter Vincent Van Gogh may have suffered from bipolar I disorder. He committed suicide at the age of 37.

hospitalization to keep the person from acting on suicidal thoughts, psychotherapy (talk therapy), sobriety (if drug and alcohol use is a factor), medication, or some combination thereof.

Occurrence of Mood Disorders

6

The lifetime prevalence of major depressive disorder is estimated to range between 15 and 20%.[12] This means that in the general population, 15–20% of people will meet the criteria for a major depressive disorder at some point in their lives. Men and women do not experience depression at the same rates—women become clinically depressed more often than men (Figure 6.1).[13] The reason for this gender disparity is most likely a combination of genetic, hormonal, and behavioral factors.

The lifetime prevalence for bipolar disorder type I is between 1 and 2%, and this disorder affects both genders equally.[14] Estimates for the prevalence of bipolar disorder type II are slightly higher, at approximately 3–5%.[15] Because bipolar disorder can be more disruptive and severe in its pathology than major depression, it is more often brought to the attention of a medical specialist, whereas millions of people with major depression never seek any kind of treatment. Because sadness and other depressive symptoms can be viewed as a part of normal life, often the people who undergo a major depressive episode don't realize that they may need treatment.

Mood disorders can occur anytime between childhood and old age. However, they do usually follow the common pattern of occurring by age 30 for bipolar disorder and by age 40 for major depressive disorder. Some experts have speculated that the occurrence of mood disorders is happening to younger and

Figure 6.1 In the general population, 15–20% of people will meet the criteria for major depressive disorder. Women have a higher risk of becoming clinically depressed than men.

younger individuals, and this may be true. Some theories for why this is occurring include the role of increased stresses faced by today's youth. Another factor may be the wider use of alcohol and illicit substances among adolescents, which can contribute to or mimic a mood disorder.

RISK FACTORS FOR MOOD DISORDERS

So, who is most likely to be afflicted with a mood disorder?

Can you tell?

Can you tell which ball is more expensive?
Which one is filled with stone?
Which one is new?

Can you tell if this person is clinically depressed?
Is she manic?
Is she suicidal?

The answer is no.

Just as you cannot judge a book by its cover, nor can you tell a person's mental state by simply looking at him or her. Although outward behavior can help, it takes observation in different situations and a detailed interview to learn what someone is feeling on the inside.

We've already mentioned that women are more likely than men to develop major depressive disorder, and that bipolar disorder remains equal between the genders. It is also an accepted fact that major depressive disorder occurs more frequently in people who are single, divorced, or separated. The same is true of bipolar disorder. The cause and effect here is not known. Does the stress of being alone cause an increased risk of developing these mood disorders? Or are people with mood disorders more likely to experience interpersonal and marital discord and therefore wind up alone? Both are probably true to some extent.

Some people consider financial success a major indicator of happiness in society. However, the data does not show a link between financial well-being and happiness. People of lower socioeconomic status are no more likely to have mood disorders than those who are wealthy. Lack of financial resources can be a huge stressor in people's lives, but it is just one facet of what makes up the complex quilt of life.

One special consideration in the recurrence of major depressive episodes is the concept of learned helplessness. Laboratory animals exhibit this phenomenon. When animals are repeatedly exposed to electric shocks without being allowed to escape, eventually they give up the effort and do not even try to escape. It is as if the lack of success gets reinforced, which gives rise to an acceptance of failure. This phenomenon is thought to be a factor in the recurrence of depressive episodes for sufferers of major depressive disorder.[16]

The Development of Mood Disorders

NEUROTRANSMITTERS

What causes mood disorders? So far, science has told us so that most mood disorders result from an imbalance in some of the neurotransmitter systems of the brain. Our brains are made up of approximately 100 billion neurons, or nerve cells, which connect with each other and through the spinal cord with the rest of the body. **Neurotransmitters** are protein substances that neurons use to communicate with each other. The different neurotransmitters in the brain include **acetylcholine**, **glutamate**, GABA, **norepinephrine**, **serotonin**, and **dopamine**. The neurotransmitters norepinephrine, serotonin, and dopamine are in the minority. Only a small fraction of the brain's neurons use these neurotransmitters to signal other cells. These three neurotransmitters, however, are very powerful. They can modulate the activity of the entire brain.

Mood disorders have been linked primarily to a dysfunction in the norepinephrine and serotonin neurotransmitter systems of the brain (Figure 7.1).[17] Norepinephrine is analogous to adrenaline for the brain—it is responsible for giving us a "zest for life." Our motiviation to get up in the morning, shower, and go to work or school comes primarily from the norepinephrine neurotransmitter system. Serotonin is a **homeostatic** neurotransmitter that impacts our sleep cycles, appetites, mood, and anxiety level. Dopamine, the third neurotransmitter, is highly

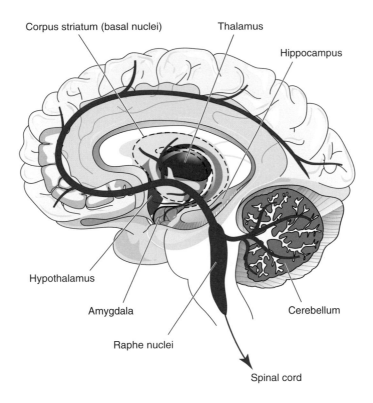

Corpus striatum (basal nuclei)   Thalamus

Hippocampus

Hypothalamus

Amygdala   Cerebellum

Raphe nuclei

Spinal cord

Figure 7.1 Mood disorders have been linked to a dysfunction in the norepinephrine and serotonin neurotransmitter systems of the brain. Serotonin is made in a small group of brain areas that are called the raphe nuclei. This view of the brain shows that the raphe nuclei form a continuous collection of cell groups throughout the brain stem. Serotonin is carried to other areas of the brain, such as the cortex, corpus striatum, and hippocampus.

associated with pleasure (as well as addictions). Eating chocolate, having sex, or using certain drugs increases dopamine activity in pleasure areas of the brain. One illustration of this biochemical link can be seen in the fact that the brain tissue of deceased people who have suffered from depression has been shown to have reduced concentrations of serotonin and its metabolites.

HORMONES

Certain biological hormones may also play a role in the development of mood disorders. These include thyroid hormone, cortisol, and steroid hormones such as **testosterone** and **estrogen**. All of these hormones originate in the **hypothalamus** and **pituitary gland**, an area of the brain that is tucked under the cortex and located squarely behind our noses.

GENETICS

There is more and more evidence today showing that genetics plays a key role in the development of mood disorders, especially bipolar disorder. **First-degree relatives** of individuals with bipolar I disorder are 10–15 times more likely to have bipolar disorder and 2–10 times more likely to have major depressive disorder, compared with control subjects (family members of individuals who do not have the condition). First-degree relatives of individuals with major depressive disorder are about twice as likely to have bipolar disorder and 2–3 times more likely to have major depressive disorder than control subjects. The **heritability** of mood disorders is also very high, even higher than general medical conditions like **heart disease**, **diabetes**, and high blood pressure. About 50% of individuals with bipolar I disorder have at least one parent with a mood disorder. Here is another striking statistic: If both parents have bipolar I disorder, their children have a greater than 50% risk of having a mood disorder.[18]

TWIN STUDIES

One way scientists have found to identify genetic and environmental factors related to a disease is to study the lives of twins. Twins come in two varieties—identical twins, who are genetically identical because they develop from one fertilized egg that splits into two embryos; and fraternal twins, who develop from two separate fertilized eggs. Fraternal twins are not identical and may just look like siblings. Identical twins, who share the same **DNA** (**deoxyribonucleic acid**), have a much higher **concordance rate** (the percentage of sets of twins where *both* twins have the disease) for mood disorders than fraternal twins. This fact argues in favor of a genetic and biological basis for mood disorders in addition to factors in the environment.

Adopted children can also help isolate genetic factors that get transplanted into a different environment. By studying adopted children, one can study the same nature versus nurture equation. Children whose biological parents suffered from mood disorders are more likely to suffer from mood disorders themselves, even when they are raised by adoptive parents who do not have mood disorders.

LIFE STRESSORS

Research is showing that genetics and biology play a vital role in the development of mood disorders. However, patient data support the assertion that a major life stressor can trigger the first episode of a mood disorder in a person's life.[19, 20] A major life stressor can be something like the death of a family member, the end of a relationship, or the loss of a job. It appears that in those people who are susceptible to a mood disorder, whether due to a genetic or biological **predisposition**, the stressful event serves as the trigger. Whereas a major life stressor can affect any normal functioning person in a serious and possibly negative way, only a certain percentage of affected individuals will meet the criteria for a mood disorder.

Major life stressors serve as triggers not just for major depressive disorder, but for bipolar disorder as well. It is not unusual for an individual to experience a manic or hypomanic episode, especially the first one, in response to a major life stressor. The link between stress and mood disorders may shed some light on possible neural mechanisms that underlie mood disorders. It is hypothesized that major stress causes a disruption of normal neurotransmitter activity in the brain. That disruption can result in either major depressive symptoms or manic or hypo-manic symptoms (although these are less common).

As stated previously, any one of many kinds of life stressors may bring on a mood episode. However, certain life events are backed up by data showing their link to a mood disorder. The stressors of losing a parent, parental divorce, or major illness during early adolescence are shown to be linked to a higher risk of developing major depressive disorder as an adult.[21,22] Scientists believe that this major stress causes long-lasting changes in the way a child's brain develops. The timing of the development of a mood disorder is also correlated with the severity of the disorder. The earlier the onset of a mood disor-der such as major depression, the more severe the illness, com-pared to a later onset.[23] Other major stressors during childhood, such as physical, sexual, or **psychological abuse**, have also been associated with psychiatric problems later in life.

FINAL ANALYSIS: A COMBINATION OF CAUSES

We exist as a sum of all of our experiences, all of our relation-ships with the people in our lives, and of the world around us. Therefore, the way one person views the world can differ greatly from how another person sees things, even though both people may come from similar families and backgrounds. People asso-ciate different meanings with different events or interactions. An event that might be mildly troublesome to one person could be devastating to another, or even considered good fortune to a third. For example, the loss of a job could be devastating to someone who is barely staying out of bankruptcy, but the same job loss might be considered a blessing in disguise for a person who was fantasizing about quitting so that he or she could go to law school. People naturally link much of their self-worth and self-esteem to the various roles they assume in life, such as in a job or within a family. When these roles become either stressed or disrupted, depression can ensue.[24] Similarly, an eighth-grader who brings home a "C" in all of his classes might be praised by his parents for passing all of his classes, whereas his peer might be grounded for ruining a 4.0 grade point average. For one person, a girlfriend or boyfriend saying the words "We need to talk" can cause a fall into heartbreak, with the end of the relationship in sight. To another, the same words may be the insignificant opening line to a simple conversation. In the end, we are all psychologically "primed" through our own experiences and upbringing. It is sometimes this priming that can help lead to the development of a mood disorder.

EXPLAINING MOOD DISORDERS: THEORIES

Many psychological theories have been developed to explain depression. For some people, when the world fails to meet expectations, serious dejection can occur. When one's wants and desires cannot be achieved within the reality of a situation, depression can ensue. Prominent psychoanalyst Edward Bibring (1895–1959) theorized that depression arises from the tension of comparing idealized aspirations to reality. Italian-American psychoanalyst Silvano Arieti (1914–1981) believed that many depressed people have lived their lives for someone else, known as the dominant other. This dominant other need not be a person. It may be an employer, an institution, or an ideal. One of the more commonly practiced and highly studied theories is that of **cognitive** theory. The word *cognitive* basically means "pertaining to thought." Therefore, this theory involves cognitive distortions, or distortions of thinking: negative distortions of life experience, negative self-evaluation, pessimism, and hopelessness. These things can both cause and perpetuate the symptoms of depression.

Treatment of Mood Disorders

The treatment of psychiatric disorders throughout much of history has often been inhumane and shameful. People with severe mental illness have been incarcerated, tortured, caged in their own homes, and even executed. In the eighteenth and nineteenth centuries, the mainstay of psychiatric treatment for the most severe cases was primarily segregation from society and custodial care. By the late nineteenth and into the twentieth century, the beginnings of biological psychiatry were taking hold. Biological treatments for mental disorders involve physically or chemically changing brain activity by manipulating neurons so that symptoms can be reduced, ultimately helping patients lead more functional lives.

INPATIENT VERSUS OUTPATIENT TREATMENT

The first decision to be made is whether a person's symptoms are severe enough to warrant inpatient psychiatric hospitalization. There are multiple benefits of psychiatric hospitalization. Inpatient treatment can provide a safe and therapeutic environment, away from outside stressors. It can allow for a more intensive interview and assessment by mental health professionals. Medical tests can readily be performed in a hospital setting. Treatment can be started quickly and its effects monitored. Whereas in the past inpatient hospitalization lasted for months, most inpatient stays today last for fewer than 14 days.

Inpatient hospitalization is usually reserved for severe forms of a mood disorder. The central factor that determines whether hospitalization is needed is the individual's potential to cause harm to him- or herself or someone else. This can either be intentional harm, such as suicide, or the harm that comes from severe debilitation (for example, not being able to care for oneself or one's dependents). This debilitation could also arise as the result of a psychotic mood disorder when a person is not able to think clearly and rationally enough to engage in outpatient treatment. Other reasons to choose hospitalization include a high level of impulsivity or a lack of insight to the point that the patient refuses treatment.

In some of the situations described above, a person may need to be temporarily "committed" to a psychiatric facility for observation and treatment. This is an involuntary process that can be carried out against the patient's will and perhaps even against the will of his or her family members. This process is only utilized when grave danger exists if the individual is left untreated (for example, someone who is imminently suicidal). Each state has slightly different laws concerning this process, but most states provide the patient with legal rights—such as a court hearing within the first few days of involuntary treatment to allow the patient to voice opposition before a judge. This is to ensure that the rights of the patient are not violated.

Inpatient hospitalization is relatively uncommon. The vast majority of individuals who receive treatment for mood disorders obtain it as outpatients. Treatment might entail therapy sessions anywhere from several times per week to once every one to three months, depending on the level of care that is needed.

PSYCHOTHERAPY

Rudimentary efforts at psychotherapy have probably existed for as long as there have been mood disorders. *Psychotherapy* is the term for any treatment that uses a therapeutic form of communication designed to achieve a certain psychological goal, which may be to identify conflicts, deal with stressors, stop distorted thinking (such as "I'm a failure"), and reduce symptoms of distress, to begin a path toward healing. This form of treatment gained fame in the late nineteenth and early twentieth centuries, in large part due to the work of Austrian physician Sigmund Freud.

Numerous types of psychotherapy are in use today. The two types of therapy that have proven to be very beneficial in the treatment of mood disorders are **cognitive-behavioral therapy** (**CBT**) and **interpersonal therapy** (**IPT**).

Cognitive-behavioral Therapy

CBT assumes that problems in a person's thoughts and behaviors contribute to depressive symptoms and, therefore, making changes in thoughts and behaviors can affect mood states. CBT places the focus of the therapy on distorted cognitions (such as "I'm worthless" or "I'll never succeed") and the emotions connected to them (such as guilt, shame, and sadness) and tries to establish associations between thoughts and behaviors that are more positive. CBT can be utilized as a short-term therapy (as little as 12 weeks) and has been shown to be as effective as antidepressants in the treatment of severe, nonpsychotic depression. There is also evidence that CBT is more effective than medication in preventing a relapse of symptoms once the treatment is completed.

Interpersonal Therapy

Interpersonal therapy, or IPT, assumes that depression occurs in an interpersonal context (the way an individual relates to other people). In IPT, by working with the interpersonal environment (using greater self-awareness and communication strategies), an improvement in depressive symptoms can be brought about.

Psychoanalysis

Psychodynamic and psychoanalytic therapies are the ones that

Sigmund Freud (1856–1939)

Sigmund Freud was a pioneer in the fields of psychiatry and psychology. He founded the psychoanalytic school of psychotherapy, which believed that unconscious drives fuel much of human behavior. He developed the theory that the unconscious mind is made up of three parts: the id, ego, and superego. The id is the most basic human drive—the one that seeks out pleasures such as sex, food, and wealth. The superego is the conscience that tries to balance out the cravings of the id by emphasizing what is morally right or socially acceptable. Finally, the ego is the mediator between the two as the mind tries to deal with external elements.

Freud was also instrumental in the development of the theory of defense mechanisms, work that was continued by his daughter, Anna Freud. Perhaps the best-known defense mechanism is denial. The purpose of defense mechanisms is to help reconcile the conflicts that are created by the constant battle between the id and the superego. It is here that Freud thought the human psyche gave rise to such conditions as hysteria, anxiety, and depression—irreconcilable conflicts between the id and superego.

Freud's theories were highly controversial at the time he introduced them and remain so to this day. Nevertheless, they have generated an immense impact not only on the mental health field, but also on the general public.

evolved directly from Sigmund Freud's work. These therapies focus on the identification of unconscious motivations for actions and the use of transference, or the reexperiencing of certain emotions and behaviors due to an unconscious connection to a past experience or relationship. Because these therapies are very individualized and require long-term treatment (psychoanalysis can take years), it is difficult to study how effective they are. Although there is no hard evidence that these strategies are effective in treating mood disorders, practitioners and patients alike praise these therapies because they help people develop a more comprehensive understanding of themselves.

PHARMACOLOGICAL TREATMENTS

The twentieth century brought great advances in biological treatments in psychiatry. The most prevalent of these interventions is the use of medications to treat psychiatric disorders. One of the first medications that emerged for treatment was **lithium**, which was found to calm agitated animals in medical experiments. Lithium is a naturally occurring salt that is found on the periodic table of chemical elements. Its use spread to psychiatric patients, and lithium remains in use today as a common treatment for bipolar disorder. Another one of the first drugs used in psychiatric treatment was **chlorpromazine** (Thorazine®) introduced in 1950, which was developed as an **anesthetic** but was also found to be useful for agitated patients. These discoveries led to an explosion of research that led to the creating or finding of hundreds of different medicinal compounds, many of which are available today. Most psychotropic medications work by targeting a **receptor** that affects the way neurons in the brain communicate with each other.

MOOD STABILIZERS

Mood stabilizers are medications that are used to treat bipolar disorder. Specifically, they have anti-manic effects and, in some cases, can prevent someone with the illness from experiencing a manic or hypomanic episode. Lithium was the first drug discovered to have mood-stabilizing effects—animals as well as humans were found to become more sedate when given lithium. Other mood stabilizers include medications that are often given to people with **seizures**. These include **valproic acid** (Depakote®), **lamotrigine** (Lamictal®), and **carbamazepine** (Tegretol®). A recent development in the treatment of bipolar disorder is the discovery that many of the medications used to treat schizophrenia are also effective in the treatment of bipolar disorder. These include **olanzapine** (Zyprexa®), **risperidone** (Risperdal®), **aripiprazole** (Abilify®), **quetiapine** (Seroquel®), and **ziprasidone** (Geodon®).

Table 8.1

SELECTIVE SEROTONIN REUPTAKE INHIBITORS (SSRIs) AND OTHER NEW GENERATION ANTIDEPRESSANTS	
BRAND NAME	GENERIC NAME
Celexa®	citalopram
Cymbalta®	duloxetine*
Effexor®	venlafaxine*
Lexapro®	escitalopram
Paxil®	paroxetine
Prozac®	fluoxetine
Remeron®	mirtazapine*
Serzone®	nefazodone
Wellbutrin®	bupropion**
Zoloft®	sertraline

* These agents are considered SNRIs—serotonin and norepinephrine reuptake inhibitors.
** Bupropion is considered an NRI—norepinephrine reuptake inhibitor.

These medications are used in the treatment of the manic episodes of bipolar disorder and many of them are also used for maintenance therapy—to prevent another manic episode. Only two of them—lithium and lamotrigine—have been clinically shown to also treat depressive episodes in bipolar patients.

Selective Serotonin Reuptake Inhibitors (SSRIs)

The **selective serotonin reuptake inhibitors,** or SSRIs, have revolutionized the pharmacological treatment of major depression and other disorders. They are the most popular category of pharmacological treatment for mood disorders and make up an industry that takes in billions of dollars every year (Table 8.1). Prozac® (fluoxetine) was the first SSRI, introduced in the late 1980s. These drugs have been found to be an effective treatment for depressive disorders, and although they may have side effects (Table 8.2), they are not considered as dangerous as older classes of anti-depressants. The use of these drugs has steadily increased since their introduction.

Another benefit of the SSRIs is that they have also become the primary treatment for most of the anxiety disorders, such as panic disorder, obsessive-compulsive disorder, generalized anxiety disorder, and posttraumatic stress disorder.

Table 8.2

SOME SIDE EFFECTS OF SSRIs*		
• dizziness	• sedation or insomnia	• change in appetite
• headache	• nausea or vomiting	• diarrhea
• sexual dysfunction	• constipation	• weight gain
* Most individuals who take SSRIs experience only minor side effects that go away with continued use of the drug.		

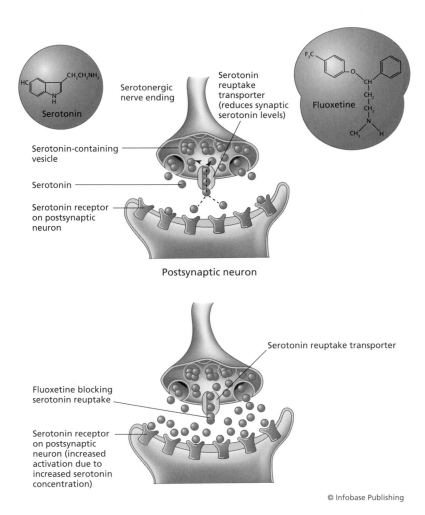

Figure 8.1 The presynaptic neuron releases serotonin into the synapse, where it binds to and activates the receptor on the postsynaptic neuron. When the receptor releases the serotonin molecule, it is taken back up into the presynaptic neuron by the serotonin reuptake transporter. SSRI drugs, such as Prozac (fluoxetine), work by blocking the activity of the reuptake transporter, thereby allowing more serotonin to remain active in the synapses for a longer period of time.

The SSRIs work by blocking the serotonin reuptake pump on the presynaptic neuron. This allows more serotonin to be available in the **synapse** and ultimately causes a **down regulation** of serotonin receptors on the postsynaptic neuron (Figure 8.1). This occurs over the period of two to five weeks and is thought to be the reason antidepressants take this much time to exert their beneficial effects.

Tricyclic Antidepressants (TCAs)

A generation of medications that stemmed from the development of chlorpromazine were the tricyclic antidepressants (TCAs), introduced in the 1950s. The clinical effect seen with these compounds was that patients became less depressed. The TCAs work by inhibiting the reuptake of norepinephrine from the synapse, thereby increasing neurotransmission. As mentioned earlier, norepinephrine is one of the neurotransmitters in the brain involved in mood regulation.

The drawbacks to using these drugs to treat depression are two-fold: the side effects they cause and the risk of heart problems. Side effects generated by these drugs may include:

- sedation
- weight gain
- blurry vision
- constipation
- urinary retention
- dizziness
- sexual dysfunction

The toxic effects usually occur at doses slightly higher than those used for the treatment of depression. They can include **cardiac arrhythmia**, seizure, coma, and death. They can be very dangerous if the drugs are used in an overdose, either accidentally or intentionally.

This class of medication is still used to treat depressive disorders (including the depressed phase of bipolar disorder), anxiety disorders, and a few other illnesses. In general, they are not typically the first choice for treatment, although some psychiatrists believe they are more potent than the newer antidepressants.

Monoamine Oxidase Inhibitors (MAOIs)

Monoamine oxidase is an enzyme found throughout the human body. Its function is to break down molecules known as **monoamines**—namely serotonin, norepinephrine, and dopamine. The **MAOIs**, as their name suggests, inhibit the function of this enzyme so that levels of the monoamine molecules rise, both in the neurons and in the synapses. The result is increased neuronal transmission wherever these molecules are found.

The MAOIs (Table 8.3) were the first pharmacological antidepressants. Easing depression was originally noted as a side effect when the drug **iproniazid** was used to treat tuberculosis, an infection of the lungs.

The MAOIs are the most complex drug therapy for the treatment of mood disorders. The reasons for this are the many side effects and drug interactions that can be very serious and sometimes lethal.

Table 8.3

THE MONOAMINE OXIDASE INHIBITORS	
BRAND NAME	**GENERIC NAME**
Parnate®	tranylcypromine
Nardil®	phenelzine
Eldepryl®	selegiline*

* Primarily used to treat Parkinson's disease; efficacy not established for depression

Hypertensive Crisis

Because of their action on norepinephrine neurotransmission throughout the body, MAOIs can cause a significant elevation of blood pressure when taken with certain drugs, or with foods that contain **tyramine**. This substance (Table 8.4) is usually broken down by the MAO enzyme, but in patients who take MAOIs, it triggers hypertensive crisis, which is indicated by flushing of the skin, elevated blood pressure, tremors, headache, shortness of breath, racing heartbeat, and elevated temperature. Certain drugs taken in combination with MAOIs, including certain over-the-counter cold remedies, may also lead to this condition.

Table 8.4

FOODS CONTAINING TYRAMINE THAT MUST BE AVOIDED WHILE ON MAOI TREATMENT	
• alcoholic beverages	• certain meats (salami, bologna, pepperoni)
• certain cheeses	
• fresh fish	• chocolate
• ginseng	• peanuts
• caffeine	

Serotonin Syndrome With MAOIs

Another very serious and potentially fatal complication of MAOIs is the risk of **serotonin syndrome**. This can occur when MAOIs are used in combination with other drugs that have serotonin activity, such as the SSRI antidepressants and other prescription medications, certain cough syrups, or the street drug **Ecstasy** (MDMA). Symptoms of serotonin syndrome include elevated temperature, high blood pressure and heart rate, seizures, heart arrhythmia, and sometimes a breakdown of muscle tissue.

Knowing these serious risks associated with MAOIs, why are these medications still used? The reason is that the way the MAOIs work is so unique—no other psychiatric drug works by irreversibly inhibiting an enzyme. Therefore, the MAOIs have been used for atypical and hard-to-treat forms of mood disorders. They are typically reserved for use as a last resort, since their use requires rigorous education and safety monitoring.

ELECTROCONVULSIVE THERAPY (ECT)

The course of medical discoveries is a fascinating study in and of itself. One such fascinating discovery has been the use of electroconvulsive therapy for major depressive disorder and other psychiatric conditions.

Did you know?

Electroconvulsive Therapy: Little-known Facts

Approximately 50,000 individuals receive ECT each year in the United States. It is used for such conditions as major depressive disorder, bipolar disorder, and schizophrenia. The usual course of treatment requires 8–12 sessions over 2–3 weeks. Each session is very short, lasting only a few minutes. Two physicians are usually present: a psychiatrist and an anesthesiologist who administers medication to prevent the patient from moving. The target organ for the electrical shock is the brain, and evidence suggests that for effective treatment a seizure in the brain for a duration of at least 30 seconds is required. Electrodes monitor brain activity during this period.

ECT may even be safer than medications for some people, such as pregnant women. It can also be more effective in treating major depressive disorder than either medications or psychotherapy, and it acts more quickly.

A neuropsychiatrist named Ladislas Joseph von Meduna discovered in 1934 that patients who suffered from epilepsy, a form of recurrent seizures, may be less likely to suffer from schizophrenia. He began to experiment with this hypothesis by inducing seizures through the use of pharmacological agents in patients with schizophrenia. By the end of the 1930s, other medical scientists had begun to use electrical current to induce seizures and started to apply this treatment to patients with mood disorders.

ECT became the treatment of choice for many serious psychiatric illnesses in the 1940s and 1950s, after which its use began to fall out of favor. The reason for this was the advent of psychiatric medications for use in depression, mania, and schizophrenia. Another reason for its rising unpopularity was public perception—it was viewed as an archaic and barbaric procedure in which a person was held down while electrical current was applied to the brain. For these reasons, as well as unflattering portrayals in the media and movies, ECT was demonized in the latter part of the twentieth century, although it did remain in use.

Today, ECT use has stabilized at a consistent level of approximately 50,000 patients a year. It has also become a very humane procedure. The patient lies virtually still for the entire procedure due to the use of sophisticated anesthetics. Contrary to public opinion, ECT is a safe and often effective, though intensive, treatment for severe mood disorders around the world (Figure 8.2).

LIGHT THERAPY (PHOTOTHERAPY)

Treatment with light therapy, also called **phototherapy**, means using an artificial light source to help influence and correct biological mechanisms (**circadian rhythms**) that affect mood and other homeostatic functions, such as sleep and appetite. The

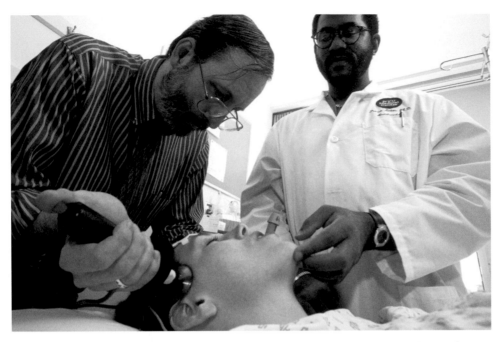

Figure 8.2 Electroconvulsive Therapy (ECT) has evolved since its early use in the 1940s and 1950s. Today, a patient lies still through the entire procedure through use of anesthetics. ECT is an effective and intense treatment for severe mood disorders.

concept came from the recognition of seasonal affective disorder. Researchers deduced that perhaps the mood changes in this illness were caused by the changes in daylight hours with different seasons. They took it one step further, realizing that treatment with light may be the answer. They were correct. Light therapy is administered by exposing the patient to a 1,500–10,000 lux light source for a period of one to four hours every day. Results are typically seen within a week (Figure 8.3).

A recent review of the research on light therapy indicates that it can be as effective as other treatments, both for seasonal affective disorder and for major depressive disorder without the seasonal component.[25]

Figure 8.3 Light therapy, also called phototherapy, requires the use of an artificial light source to help stabilize circadian rhythms that affect mood. Light therapy is administered by exposing a patient to a 1,500–10,000 lux light source for one to four hours per day.

REPETITIVE TRANSCRANIAL MAGNETIC STIMULATION (rTMS)

A promising new form of treatment for mood disorders and possibly for other conditions such as schizophrenia and **Parkinson's disease** is **repetitive transcranial magnetic stimulation (rTMS)**. It uses the same technology as that used in an MRI (magnetic resonance imaging) scan. In rTMS, a magnet is placed above the head and its magnetic field is focused on a certain area of the brain. It has been approved for use in other countries, such as Canada, for the treatment of major depressive disorder. Although it is not yet approved for use in the United States, rTMS treatments for 30 minutes each day for 2 to 4 weeks is recommended for the treatment of major depressive disorder.

There seem to be very limited side effects with this form of treatment—usually only a mild headache and transient light-headedness. Because of this, and the fact that this is an outpatient procedure that requires no anesthetic or sedation, it is an attractive alternative to pharmacological treatments or electro-convulsive therapy. Studies are currently under way to explore the potential for this new treatment in the United States.

EXERCISE THERAPY

Several studies have shown that a regimen of regular aerobic exercise has mood-lifting effects. One study showed that for nonpsychotic and nonsuicidal individuals with major depressive disorder, 30 minutes of continuous aerobic exercise 3 times per week for 16 weeks was as effective a treatment as the common antidepressant sertraline (Zoloft®).[26] However, physical exercise carries risks and is not appropriate for everyone. Certain medical conditions, such as orthopedic injuries, bone and joint problems, and heart or lung problems, can prevent individuals from exercising. People starting an exercise regimen should consult with their health-care provider.

VAGAL NERVE STIMULATION (VNS)

Vagal nerve stimulation, or VNS, was approved in 2005 by the U.S. Food and Drug Administration (FDA) for use in patients with major depressive disorder. VNS has existed as a treatment for epilepsy since 1997 and has been found to have mood benefits as well. VNS is an invasive procedure that requires the surgical implantation of an electronic device (Figure 8.4). This device sends electrical impulses into the left vagus nerve and up to the brain. VNS has been used in more than 20,000 people to treat epilepsy and is considered a treatment of last resort—one that is used when other, more common, forms of treatment have failed.

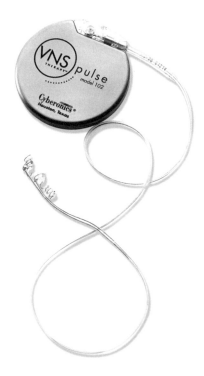

Figure 8.4 Vagal nerve stimulation (VNS) requires the surgical implantation of an electronic device (shown here) to send electrical impulses to the brain. VNS is usually used to treat epilepsy but has also been used to treat major depressive disorder.

SUMMARY

Rare but universal side effects exist with all forms of treatment for depression, including ECT medications and light therapy, which may induce a switch to a manic state. A small percentage of individuals who are undergoing treatment will progress into hypomania or mania. It is as if the treatment is analogous to a foot gently pushing on an accelerator, but, in some cases, this causes the car to race. This is a serious complication and demands immediate medical attention. Some people who undergo this side effect may actually have bipolar disorder and be misdiagnosed with major depressive disorder.

The treatment of a mood disorder can be a complex medical decision to be made by a patient with his or her health-care provider. There is no one treatment for mood disorders that will work for everyone. A treatment regimen has to be an individualized intervention recommended by a trained professional.

Millions of people have benefited from the treatments described above, either alone or in combination. The important message is that there *is* treatment. No longer do people have to suffer for weeks, months, or years with a devastating illness that deprives them of their ability to function, their relationships with loved ones, and their happiness.

1. Thomas A. Widiger and L.M. Sankis, "Adult Psychopathology: Issues and Controversies," *Annual Review of Psychology* 51 (2000): 377–404.

2. Allen Frances and Ruth Ross, "Mood Disorders," DSM-IV-TR Case Studies: a Clinical Guide to Differential Diagnosis, ed. Ruth Ross. Washington, DC: American Psychiatric Press, 2001, pp. 120–121.

3. Allen Frances and Ruth Ross, "Mood Disorders," DSM-IV-TR Case Studies: a Clinical Guide to Differential Diagnosis, ed. Ruth Ross. Washington, DC: American Psychiatric Press, 2001, pp. 110–111.

4. Allen Frances and Ruth Ross, "Mood Disorders," DSM-IV-TR Case Studies: a Clinical Guide to Differential Diagnosis, ed. Ruth Ross. Washington, DC: American Psychiatric Press, 2001, pp. 128–130.

5. Allen Frances and Ruth Ross, "Mood Disorders," DSM-IV-TR Case Studies: a Clinical Guide to Differential Diagnosis, ed. Ruth Ross. Washington, DC: American Psychiatric Press, 2001, pp. 135–136.

6. Allen Frances and Ruth Ross, "Mood Disorders," DSM-IV-TR Case Studies: a Clinical Guide to Differential Diagnosis, ed. Ruth Ross. Washington, DC: American Psychiatric Press, 2001, p. 140.

7. Allen Frances and Ruth Ross, "Mood Disorders," DSM-IV-TR Case Studies: a Clinical Guide to Differential Diagnosis, ed. Ruth Ross. Washington, DC: American Psychiatric Press, 2001, pp. 142–144.

8. Allen Frances and Ruth Ross, "Mood Disorders," DSM-IV-TR Case Studies: a Clinical Guide to Differential Diagnosis, ed. Ruth Ross. Washington, DC: American Psychiatric Press, 2001, pp. 148–149.

9. World Health Organization, "World Health Organization—Mental Health," *World Health Organization.* Available online at http://www.who.int/mental_health/en.

10. Thomas E. Joiner, Jr., Jessica S. Brown, and LaRicka R. Wingate, "The Psychology and Neurobiology of Suicidal Behavior," *Annual Review of Psychology* 56 (2005): 287–314.

11. Joiner, et al, 2005.

12. B. Birmaher, N.D. Ryan, D.E. Williamson, D.A. Brent, J. Kaufman, R. E. Dahl, et al., "Childhood and Adolescent Depression: A Review of the Past 10 Years. Part I," *Journal of the Academy of Child and Adolescent Psychiatry* 35 (1996): 1427–1439.

13. R.C. Kessler, K.A. McGonagle, M. Swartz, D.G. Blazer, & G.B. Nelson, "Sex and Depression in the National Comorbidity Survey, I: lifetime prevalence, chronicity and recurrence," *Journal of Affective Disorders* 29 (1993): 85–96.

14. J.R. Alexander, J. Benjamin, B. Lerer, M. Baron, and R.H. Belmaker, "Frequency of Positive Family History in Bipolar Patients in a Catchment-Area Population," *Progress in Neuro-Psychopharmacology & Biological Psychiatry* 119 (1995): 367–373.

15. Michael Berk and Seetal Dodd, "Bipolar II Disorder: A Review," *Bipolar Disorders* 7 (2005): 11–21.

16. Lyn Y. Abramson, Martin E. Seligman, and John D. Teasdale, "Learned Helplessness in Humans: Critique and

Reformulation," *Journal of Abnormal Psychology* 87 (1978): 49–74.

17. Richard J. Davidson, Diego Pizzagalli, Jack B. Nitchke, and Katherine Putnam, "Depression: Perspectives from Affective Neuroscience," *Annual Review of Psychology* Volume 53 (2000): 545–574.

18. Harold I. Kaplan and Benjamin J. Sadock, "Major Depressive Disorder, Bipolar I Disorder, and Bipolar II Disorder," *Synopsis of Psychiatry*, 8th ed., ed. Robert Cancro. Baltimore, MD: Williams & Wilkins, 1998, pp. 538–543.

19. Birmaher, et al, 1996.

20. Ronald C. Kessler, "The Effects of Stressful Live Events on Depression," *Annual Review of Psychology* 48 (1997): 191–214.

21. David S. Bennett and John E. Bates, "Prospective models of depressive symptoms in early adolescence: Attributional style, stress, and support," *Journal of Early Adolescence* 15 (1995): 299–315.

22. Benjamin L. Hankin and Lyn Y. Abramson, "Development of gender differences in depression: An elaborated cognitive vulnerability-transactional stress theory," *Psychological Bulletin* 127 (2001): 773–796.

23. Bruce E. Compas, Sydney Ey, and Katherine E. Grant, "Taxonomy, assessment, and diagnosis of depression during adolescence," *Psychological Bulletin* 114 (1993): 323–344.

24. Keith Oatley and Winifred Bolton, "A Social-Cognitive Theory of Depression in Reaction to Life Events," *Psychological Review* 92 (1985): 372–388.

25. Robert N. Golden, Bradley N. Gaynes, R. David Ekstrom, Robert M. Hamer, Frederick M. Jacobsen, Trisha Suppes, Katherine L. Wisner, and Charles B. Nemeroff. "The Efficacy of Light Therapy in the Treatment of Mood Disorders: A Review and Meta-Analysis of the Evidence," *American Journal of Psychiatry* 162:4 (2005): 656–662.

26. Michael Babyak, James A. Blumenthal, Steve Herman, Parinda Khatri, Murali Doraiswamy, Kathleen Moore, W. Edward Craighead, Teri T. Baldewicz, and K. Ranga Krishnan. "Exercise Treatment for Major Depression: Maintenance of Therapeutic Benefit at 10 Months," *Psychosomatic Medicine* 62 (2000): 633–638.

Acetylcholine—An excitatory protein substance found throughout the body and the brain that functions as a signal for nerve cells.

Adjustment disorder—A psychiatric diagnosis characterized by conduct changes or symptoms of mood or anxiety in response to an identifiable stressor.

Androgen—A steroid hormone that controls the development of masculine characteristics.

Anesthesiologist—A physician who specializes in the administration of medication to alter consciousness so as to relieve pain, such as during surgical operations.

Anesthetic—Medication used to ease pain or alter consciousness; primarily used during medical procedures.

Antidepressant—A class of medication used to treat symptoms of depression.

Aripiprazole (**Abilify®**)—A medication used for the treatment of bipolar disorder and schizophrenia.

Attention-deficit/hyperactivity disorder (**ADHD**)—A psychiatric disorder characterized by impulsivity, hyperactivity, and a lack of the ability to focus one's attention.

Bereavement—The process of grief that follows a major loss, such as the death of a loved one.

Bipolar I disorder—A psychiatric mood disorder characterized by alternating episodes of mania, or pathologically elevated mood, and major depressive episodes; this is the most severe form of bipolar disorder.

Bipolar II disorder—A psychiatric mood disorder characterized by alternating episodes of hypomania, or pathologically elevated mood, and major depressive episodes; this is a milder form of bipolar disorder.

Brief psychotic disorder—A psychiatric disorder characterized by hallucinations, disorganized speech, or delusions of thought that last less than one month.

Carbamazepine (**Tegretol®**)—A medication that has been used to treat epilepsy, certain types of pain, and bipolar disorder.

Cardiac arrhythmia—An abnormal rhythm of the heart that can cause dizziness, fainting, loss of consciousness, and death.

Cerebrospinal fluid—The watery liquid that bathes the brain and spinal cord in the central nervous system.

Chlorpromazine (Thorazine®)—A medication that has been used to treat schizophrenia; it was the first medication discovered to treat this condition.

Circadian rhythm—A daily cycle of activity exhibited by organisms based on daylight.

Clinical depression—A depressed state severe enough to require intervention from a medical professional.

Cognitive—Relating to thinking or thought processes.

Cognitive-behavioral therapy (CBT)—A type of psychotherapy that helps identify and correct distorted thought patterns and engages in enacting behavioral changes to challenge those thought patterns.

Concordance rate—The rate at which the same trait is found in a pair of twins.

Cortisol—A hormone produced by the adrenal glands that regulates carbohydrate metabolism and maintains blood pressure.

Cyclothymic disorder—A psychiatric mood disorder characterized by alternating episodes of elation, hyperactivity, and depression; this is the mildest form of the bipolar disorders.

Defense mechanism—An unconscious mechanism by which the mind tries to prevent itself from feeling shame, guilt, anxiety, or another negative emotion.

Delusion—A fixed but false belief that is outside the realm of normal thinking for a particular population or culture and continues to remain active despite evidence that it is incorrect.

Delusional disorder—A psychiatric disorder characterized primarily by delusional thought patterns.

Diabetes (also known as diabetes mellitus)—An endocrinological disorder that causes a dysfunction of blood sugar regulation.

DNA (deoxyribonucleic acid)—A nucleic acid that contains genetic instructions for all living cellular organisms.

Dopamine—An excitatory or inhibitory protein substance found throughout the body and the brain that functions as a signal for nerve cells; it is involved in the perception of pleasure in the brain.

Down-regulation—The process by which a human cell can self-regulate its function by decreasing a facet of its physiology, such as by decreasing the concentration of chemical messenger receptors on its surface.

Dysfunction—Abnormal function.

Ecstasy—A type of illegally abused amphetamine that has hallucinatory properties; its full name is methylene-dioxy-methamphetamine (MDMA).

Ego—One of the three parts of the mind; it is conscious and interacts with the outside world.

Elation—Extreme joy; euphoria.

Electroconvulsive therapy (**ECT**)—A type of psychiatric treatment that involves using an electrical current to trigger a seizure under controlled circumstances.

Epilepsy—A neurological disorder that can cause excessive electrical activity in the brain; it may consist of muscle convulsions or sometimes blank staring spells.

Estradiol—A steroid hormone produced by the ovaries.

Estrogen—A steroid hormone produced by the ovaries and intended to develop and maintain female sex characteristics.

Euphoria—Intense joy or happiness; elation.

Fatigue—A feeling of tiredness; lack of energy.

First-degree relatives—Parents, siblings, or children of an individual.

Flight of ideas—A psychological state that involves the rapid succession of thoughts about different topics that are not necessarily connected.

Glutamate—An excitatory protein substance found throughout the body and the brain that functions as a signal for nerve cells.

Grandiose—Characterized by greatness of scope or intent; can sometimes reach a delusional level.

Hallucination—A sensory perception that exists only in the mind, not in reality; can affect any of the senses.

Heart disease—A medical condition referring to a narrowing of the arteries that causes insufficient oxygen delivery to the heart; also called coronary artery disease.

Heritability—Capability of being passed from one generation to the next.

Homeostaticity—Referring to homeostesis, the process of keeping the body in balance in terms of temperature, nutrition, and other factors needed to keep the body stable.

Hypomanic episode—A mood episode that lasts at least several days and is characterized by elevated mood, increased energy, decreased need for sleep, flight of ideas, and impulsivity; less severe than a manic episode; usually representative of bipolar II disorder or cyclothymic disorder; also called hypomania.

Hypothalamus—A part of the brain involved in regulating bodily processes such as maintaining proper body temperature.

Id—One of the three parts of the mind responsible for the unconscious pursuit of pleasurable biological drives without regard to consequences.

Insomnia—An inability to obtain an adequate amount of sleep.

Interpersonal therapy (**IPT**)—A type of psychotherapy that focuses on how an individual relates to other people.

Iproniazid—A medicine developed in the 1950s, used to treat tuberculosis and also found to have antidepressant properties.

Lamotrigine (**Lamictal®**)—A medication used to treat epilepsy and bipolar disorder.

Lethargy—Extreme tiredness; fatigue.

Light therapy—A form of treatment for depression that involves using bright light for several hours each day; also known as phototherapy.

Lithium—A naturally occurring salt that is used as mood-stabilizing treatment for bipolar disorder.

Major depressive disorder—A psychiatric mood disorder characterized by at least two weeks' worth of prominent depressive symptoms such as sadness, low energy, loss of appetite, lack of pleasure or interest, excessive guilt, thoughts of suicide, or sleep disruption; at least five symptoms are needed to make a diagnosis.

Major depressive episode—A mood episode characterized by at least two weeks' worth of prominent depressive symptoms such as sadness, low energy, loss of appetite, lack of pleasure or interest, excessive guilt, thoughts of suicide, or sleep disruption; at least five symptoms are needed to make a diagnosis.

Manic depression—An old term for bipolar disorder.

Manic episode—A mood episode lasting at least a week and characterized by elevated mood, increased energy, hyperactivity, decreased need for sleep, flight of ideas and impulsivity; is more severe than a hypomanic episode; usually representative of bipolar I disorder; also known as mania.

MAOI—See *Monoamine oxidase inhibitor*.

Melancholia—A severe depression involving guilt, social withdrawal, and hopelessness.

Mixed episode—A mood episode that usually occurs in bipolar disorder and shares features of both a manic (or hypomanic) episode and a major depressive episode.

Monoamine—A class of compounds used by nerve cells to signal one another; included are norepinephrine, serotonin, and dopamine.

Monoamine oxidase—An enzyme used in nerve cells to break down the monoamine compounds norepinephrine, serotonin, and dopamine.

Monoamine oxidase inhibitor (**MAOI**)—A medication that inhibits the enzyme monoamine oxidase.

Mood disorder due to general medical condition—A type of mood disorder characterized by depressive symptoms that are caused directly by the biological activity of another disease.

Mood stabilizer—A class of medications used to treat the manic or hypomanic episodes of bipolar disorder.

Neurotransmitter—A protein substance used by nerve cells to signal each other.

Norepinephrine—An excitatory protein substance found throughout the body and the brain that functions as a signal for nerve cells; involved in the regulation of various aspects of mood.

Olanzapine (**Zyprexa**®)—A medication used to treat bipolar disorder and schizophrenia.

Parkinson's disease—A neurological disease that causes a depletion of dopamine in a part of the brain that controls movement; this disease causes slow movements and tremors.

Phototherapy—See *Light therapy.*

Pituitary gland—A gland in the brain that secretes various hormones that act in other parts of the body.

Postpartum blues—Short-lived feelings of sadness that are mild and affect women during the period after childbirth.

Postpartum depression—A mood disorder that is characterized by a major depressive episode that occurs in the weeks or months after a woman gives birth to a child.

Predisposition—A tendency or susceptibility.

Prevalence—The total number of cases of a disease at a given point in time.

Progesterone—A steroid sex hormone secreted by the ovaries.

Prognosis—A prediction of the future outcome of a disease.

Psychiatry—The medical specialty devoted to the diagnosis, treatment, and prevention of mental illnesses such as bipolar disorder, schizophrenia, and major depressive disorder.

Psychological abuse—A pattern of repeated intimidation and control of an individual through criticism, harsh words, or the threat of harm.

Psychotherapy—A form of treatment that involves using psychological techniques through communication to help identify symptoms and conflicts, change behaviors, and improve overall functioning.

Psychotic features—Psychiatric symptoms that reveal a lack of a sense of reality including delusions and hallucinations; also called psychosis.

Quetiapine (Seroquel®)—A medication used for psychiatric disorders, including schizophrenia and bipolar disorder.

Receptor—Highly specific protein structure located throughout the body that initiates biological activity when stimulated by a specific substance such as a hormone, drug, or neurotransmitter.

Repetitive transcranial magnetic stimulation (rTMS)—A form of treatment that uses a magnetized coil to induce changes in the brain to relieve symptoms, such as those that occur with depression.

Risperidone (**Risperdal®**)—A medication used for psychiatric disorders, including schizophrenia and bipolar disorder.

Schizoaffective disorder—A psychiatric disorder characterized by features of either major depressive disorder or bipolar disorder, in combination with schizophrenia.

Schizophrenia—A psychiatric disorder characterized by dissociation from reality, delusions, and hallucinations.

Seasonal affective disorder (**SAD**)—A subtype of the psychiatric illness major depressive disorder, characterized by symptoms of major depression that occur seasonally.

Seizure—A neurological event that occurs due to excessive electrical activity in the brain and can cause muscular convulsions, staring spells, and loss of consciousness.

Selective serotonin reuptake inhibitor (**SSRI**)—A class of medications used to treat mood and anxiety disorders; these drugs work by blocking the serotonin reuptake pump on nerve cell endings.

Serotonin—An excitatory protein substance found throughout the body and the brain that functions as a signal for nerve cells; involved in the regulation of various aspects of mood and anxiety.

Serotonin syndrome—A medical complication caused by excessive medications or from drug-drug interactions; symptoms include fever, muscle rigidity, nausea, vomiting, and disorientation.

Substance-induced mood disorder—A mood disorder characterized by manic, hypomanic, or depressive mood symptoms that occur due to the ingestion of a substance, drug, or medication.

Superego—One of the three parts of the mind, which serves as an authority figure to place moral and ethical restrictions on one's behavior.

Synapse—The space between nerve cells where neurotransmitters (signaling proteins) are used by the nerve cells to send a signal.

Testosterone—A steroid sex hormone produced by the testes and responsible for the development and maintenance of male secondary sex characteristics.

Tyramine—A protein found in certain foods that can cause medical complications when consumed with the antidepressants known as monoamine oxidase inhibitors (MAOIs).

Vagal nerve stimulation (**VNS**)—A medical treatment used for epilepsy and major depressive disorder that involves implantation of a device in the body that rhythmically stimulates the vagus nerve.

Valproic acid (**Depakote®**)—A medication used to treat epilepsy and bipolar disorder.

Ziprasidone (**Geodon®**)—A medication used to treat bipolar disorder and schizophrenia.

American Psychiatric Association. *Diagnostic and Statistical Manual of Mental Disorders*, 4th ed. Washington, D.C.: American Psychiatric Press, 2000.

———. *Diagnostic and Statistical Manual of Mental Disorders, Fourth Edition Text Revision Case Studies: A Clinical Guide to Differential Diagnosis*. Washington, D.C.: American Psychiatric Press, 2001.

Andreasen, Nancy C., and Donald W. Black. *Introductory Textbook of Psychiatry*, 3rd ed. Washington, D.C.: American Psychiatric Press, 2001.

Beyer, John L., Richard D. Weiner, and Mark D. Glenn. *Electroconvulsive Therapy: A Programmed Text*, 2nd ed. Washington, D.C.: American Psychiatric Press, 1998.

Dubuc, Bruno. "The Brain from Top to Bottom." *McGill University*. Available online at *http://www.thebrain.mcgill.ca/*.

Ebert, Michael H., Peter T. Loosen, and Barry Nurcombe. *Current Diagnosis & Treatment in Psychiatry*. New York: Lange Medical Books/McGraw-Hill, 2000.

Harmon, Daniel E. *The Tortured Mind: The Many Faces of Manic Depression*. Philadelphia: Chelsea House Publishers, 2000.

Kaplan, Harold I., and Benjamin J. Sadock. *Synopsis of Psychiatry*, 8th ed. Baltimore: Williams & Wilkins, 1998.

National Alliance for the Mentally Ill. "People with Mental Illness Enrich our Lives." *National Alliance for the Mentally Ill*. Available online at *http://www.nami.org/Template.cfm?Section=Helpline1&template=/ ContentManagement/ContentDisplay.cfm&ContentID=4858*.

Pauley, Jane. "Jane Pauley Shares Her Story." *MSNBC*. Available online at *http://msnbc.msn.com/id/5887567/*.

Sadock, Benjamin J., and Virginia A. Sadock. *Kaplan & Sadock's Comprehensive Textbook of Psychiatry*, 7th ed. Philadelphia: Lippincott Williams & Wilkins, 2000.

Shields, Brooke. "Brooke Shields Battles Postpartum Depression,"

MSNBC. Available online at *http://www.msnbc.msn.com/id/7748616/*.

Shorter, Edward. *A History of Psychiatry: From the Era of the Asylum to the Age of Prozac*. New York: John Wiley & Sons, Inc., 1997

Stahl, Stephen. *Essential Psychopharmacology: Neuroscientific Basis and Practical Applications*. Cambridge, United Kingdom: Cambridge University Press, 1996.

Stern, Theodore A., and John B. Herman. *Psychiatry Update & Board Preparation*. New York: McGraw-Hill, 2004.

Vincent van Gogh Gallery. "Vincent van Gogh: Biography." *Vincent van Gogh Gallery*. Available online at *http://www.vangoghgallery.com/misc/bio.htm*

Arena, Jillayne. *Step Back from the Exit: 45 Reasons to Say No to Suicide.* Milwaukee: Zebulon Press, 1996.

Blauner, Susan Rose. *How I Stayed Alive When My Brain Was Trying to Kill Me: One Person's Guide to Suicide Prevention.* New York: William Morrow, 2002.

Cobain, Bev. *When Nothing Matters Anymore: A Survival Guide for Depressed Teens.* Minneapolis: Free Spirit Publishing, 1998.

Copeland, Mary Ellen, and Stuart Copans. *Recovering from Depression: A Workbook for Teens.* Baltimore: Brookes Publishing Company, 2002.

Cytryn, Leon, and Donald H. McKnew. *Growing Up Sad: Childhood Depression and Its Treatment.* New York: W. W. Norton & Company, 1998.

Jamison, Kay Redfield. *An Unquiet Mind: A Memoir of Moods and Madness.* New York: Vintage, 1997.

———. *Night Falls Fast: Understanding Suicide.* New York: Vintage, 2000.

Kaufman, Miriam. *Overcoming Teen Depression: A Guide for Parents.* Tonawanda, NY: Firefly Books Ltd., 2001.

Klebanoff, Susan, Ellen Luborsky, and Andy Cooke. *Ups & Downs: How to Beat the Blues and Teen Depression.* Los Angeles: Price Stern Sloan, 1999.

Koplewicz, Harold. *More Than Moody: Recognizing and Treating Adolescent Depression.* New York: Perigee Books, 2003.

Machoian, Lisa. *The Disappearing Girl: Learning the Language of Teenage Depression.* New York: Dutton Adult, 2005.

Miklowitz, David J. *The Bipolar Disorder Survival Guide: What You and Your Family Need to Know.* New York: The Guilford Press, 2002.

Papolos, Demitri, and Janice Papolos. *The Bipolar Child: The Definitive and Reassuring Guide to Childhood's Most Misunderstood Disorder.* New York: Broadway, 2000.

Styron, William. *Darkness Visible: A Memoir of Madness.* New York: Vintage, 1992.

WEBSITES

American Psychiatrtic Association: Healthy Minds
www.healthyminds.org
Child & Adolescent Bipolar Foundation
www.bpkids.org
Depression and Bipolar Support Alliance
www.dbsalliance.org
Find a Suicide Hotline in your city or state
www.suicidehotlines.com
National Alliance for the Mentally III
www.nami.org
National Institute of Mental Health
www.nimh.nih.gov
National Mental Health Association
www.nmha.org
National Mental Health Information Center
www.mentalhealth.samhsa.gov
National Strategy for Suicide Prevention
www.mentalhealth.samhsa.gov/suicideprevention
National Youth Network
www.nationalyouth.com
Suicide Awareness Voices of Education
www.save.org

Abilify is a registered trademark of Otsuka America Pharmaceutical, Inc.; Celexa is a registered trademark of Forest Pharmaceuticals, Inc.; Cymbalta is a registered trademark of Eli Lilly and Company; Depakote is a registered trademark of Abbott Laboratories; Effexor is a registered trademark of Wyeth Pharmaceuticals Inc.; Eldepryl is a registered trademark of Somerset Pharmaceuticals, Inc.; Geodon is a registered trademark of Pfizer Inc.; Lamictal is a registered trademark of GlaxoSmithKline; Lexapro is a registered trademark of Forest Pharmaceuticals, Inc.; Nardil is a registered trademark of Pfizer Inc.; Parnate is a registered trademark of GlaxoSmithKline; Paxil is a registered trademark of GlaxoSmithKline; Prozac is a registered trademark of Eli Lilly and Company; Remeron is a registered trademark of Organon USA Inc.; Risperdal is a registered trademark of Janssen, L.P.; Ritalin is a registered trademark of Novartis Pharmaceuticals; Seroquel is a registered trademark of AstraZeneca Pharmaceuticals, L.P.; Serzone is a registered trademark of Bristol-Myers Squibb Company; Tegretol is a registered trademark of Novartis Pharmaceuticals; Thorazine is a registered trademark of SmithKline Beecham; Wellbutrin is a registered trademark of GlaxoSmithKline; Zoloft is a registered trademark of Pfizer Inc.; Zyprexa is a registered trademark of Eli Lilly and Company.

INDEX

Abilify® (Aripiprazole), 66
Abuse
  and mood disorders, 59
Acetylcholine, 55
ADHD. *See* Attention-deficit/hyperactivity
    disorder
Adjustment disorders, 37
Adolescent depression, 12
Alcoholism, 15
  and mood disorders, 36–37, 42–44, 52
Aldrin, Buzz, 5, 29
American Psychiatric Association (APA), 7
Androgens, 33
Antidepressant medications, 5, 11–12
  classes of, 67–72
Antipsychotic medications, 15
Anxiety disorders, 64
  treatment of, 67, 69
APA. *See* American Psychiatric Association
Arieti, Silvano, 60
Aripiprazole. *See* Abilify®
Attention-deficit/hyperactivity disorder
    (ADHD), 32

Bereavement, 37
Bibring, Edward, 60
Bipolar disorder, 36, 40
  case studies, 21–25, 27–28, 30–32
  defined, 18
  public figures with, 5, 26, 29, 48–49
  at risk, 58
  statistics, 51, 57
  symptoms of, 8, 18–22, 24–33, 35, 41,
    44, 58–59, 67, 73, 77–78
  treatment for, 21–26, 28–29, 41, 65–67,
    69, 72–73
  types, 18–32, 51, 54
Brief psychotic disorder, 13

Carbamazepine. *See* Tegretol®
Carey, Drew, 5, 16
CBT. *See* Cognitive-behavioral therapy

Celsus, Aulus Cornelius, 2, 4
Childhood bipolar disorder, 32
Chlorpromazine. *See* Thorazine®
Circadian rhythms, 73, 75
Cognitive-behavioral therapy (CBT), 63
Cognitive theories, 60
Cortisol, 39, 57
Crow, Sheryl, 5–6, 16
Cyclothymic disorder, 18
  case study, 30–32
  symptoms, 32

Delusional disorder, 13
Deoxyribonucleic acid (DNA), 58
Depakote® (valproic acid)
  treatment of bipolar disorder, 24, 66
Depression. *See* Major depressive disorder,
    and Mood disorders
Diagnosis, mood disorders
  criteria, 5–7, 9, 13, 23, 24, 29–31, 51–52,
    58
  history, 7, 36, 40–41
  interview, 7
  observation, 7, 53
  steps, 40–41
*Diagnostic and Statistical Manual, 4th edi-
    tion* (DSM-IV)
  disease classifications, 7, 13, 18
DNA. *See* Deoxyribonucleic acid
Dopamine
  function, 55–56
Down Came the Rain (Shields), 33–34
DSM-IV. *See Diagnostic and Statistical
    Manual, 4th edition*
Dysthymic disorder, 9

Ecstasy (MDMA), 71
ECT. *See* Electroconvulsive therapy
Eldepryl® (selegiline), 70
Electroconvulsive therapy (ECT), 15
  treatment for mood disorders, 72–74,
    76–77

Epilepsy, 39, 73, 76–77
Estradiol, 33
Estrogen, 57
Euthymic mood, 3
Exercise therapy, 76

FDA. *See* Food and Drug Administration
Fluoxetine. *See* Prozac®
Food and Drug Administration (FDA), 76
Freud, Anna, 64
Freud, Sigmund, 63–65

GABA, 55
Gaussian distribution curve, 3–4
Genetics
    and mood disorders, 57–58
    and suicide, 45
Geodon® (Ziprasidone), 66
Glutamate, 55

Hemingway, Ernest, 15
Hippocrates, 2
Hormones
    and mood disorders, 39, 55
Hypertensive crisis, 71
Hypomanic episodes
    features of, 18–19, 25, 27–32, 41, 58–59,
        77–78
Hypothalamus, 57
Hysteria, 64

Interpersonal therapy (IPT), 63
Iproniazid, 70
IPT. *See* Interpersonal therapy

Kraepelin, Emil, 4–5

Lamictal® (Lamotrigine), 66–67
Lamotrigine. *See* Lamictal®
Light therapy. *See* Phototherapy
Lithium
    and bipolar disorder, 26, 65–67

Major depressive disorder, 1, 5, 36, 39
    case study, 10–11
    public features of, 15–16
    at risk, 54, 58
    statistics, 51–52
    symptoms of, 7–13, 15, 17, 25, 28, 30,
        35, 39–40, 43, 54, 59–60, 64
    treatments for, 5, 11–12, 15, 29, 33–35,
        41, 51, 61–78
Major depressive disorder with psychotic
        features, 22
    case study, 14–17
    symptoms of, 13–17, 25, 33, 35, 42
    treatments for, 15, 17, 62
Major depressive episode, 1
    features, 9, 32
Mania, 2, 4, 53
    debilitating forms of, 5
    features, 1, 8, 18–21, 28, 32, 34, 39, 41,
        44, 58–59, 67, 77–78
    treatments for, 21, 73
Manic depression, 18
Manic psychosis, 5
MDMA. *See* Ecstasy
Meduna, Ladislas Joseph von, 73
Melancholia, 2
Mixed episodes
    symptoms of, 21, 41
Monoamine oxidase, 70
Monoamine Oxidase Inhibitors (MAOIs)
    action, 70–71
    complications, 71–72
    drug and food interactions, 70–71
    side effects, 70
    treatment of depression, 70–72
Mood disorders, *see also* specific types
    causes of, 55–60
    changing face of, 5
    defined, 6–7
    occurrence of, 51–54
    risk factors, 52, 54
    symptoms of, 6–8

page:

2: Scherer Illustration
4: Scherer Illustration
6: © Associated Press, AP
12: © Associated Press, AP
16: © Associated Press, AP
19: Scherer Illustration
25: Scherer Illustration
26: © Associated Press, AP
31: Scherer Illustration
34: © Associated Press, ARROYO

35: © Associated Press, NJ DEP
HEALTH SENIOR SERVICES
49: © Gianni Dagli Orti/CORBIS
52: © Associated Press, AP
56: © HFS Imaging
68: © HFS Imaging
74: © Najlah Feanny/CORBIS
75: © Louie Psihoyos/CORBIS
77: © Cyberonics/Handout/Reuters/
CORBIS

AUTHOR

Vatsal G. Thakkar, M.D., is an assistant professor of psychiatry at Vanderbilt University School of Medicine. Thakkar received his bachelor's degree from the University of Tennessee in Knoxville and his doctor of medicine from the University of Tennessee in Memphis. He currently is the medical director for the Vanderbilt Mental Health Center, where he spends his time supervising residents in outpatient practice and directing a course for second-year medical students. He specializes in the outpatient treatment of depression. Outside of psychiatry, Thakkar engages in professional photography. His most recent exhibit, entitled *Fortitude*, consists of portraits of cancer survivors. It hangs at the Vanderbilt-Ingram Cancer Center.